The Glory of His Life

The Glory Of His Life

WATCHMAN NEE

Translated from the Chinese

Christian Fellowship Publishers, Inc.
New York

Available from the Publishers at:
11515 Allecingie Parkway
Richmond, Virginia 23235

PRINTED IN U.S.A.

TRANSLATOR'S PREFACE

"When Christ, who is our life, shall be manifested, then shall ye also with him be manifested in glory" (Col. 3.4). Where the life of Christ is, there is the manifestation of glory. Though the full manifestation is yet to come, we may enjoy the glory of His life even now.

In this volume, which is a selection of messages culled from many given by Watchman Nee throughout his long years of faithful ministry to the church, we are enabled to see some of the manifold aspects of the glory of the life of Christ in us. Part I shows us how the righteousness of God has been manifested towards all who believe through faith in Jesus Christ. Further, we are shown how Christ is made our righteousness, and how as a result we become the righteousness of God. Part II proceeds to disclose how Christ is made to be our wisdom—a wisdom which includes not only righteousness but also sanctification and redemption. While Part III concludes with an unveiling of the meaning of resurrection and the power of His resurrection.

This book is presented as a companion volume to the author's *Practical Issues of This Life*.* As this life of ours has its many problems, so the life of Christ in us transcends and translates them into glory.

---

* Watchman Nee, *Practical Issues of This Life*. New York, Christian Fellowship Publishers, 1975. Translated from the Chinese.

CONTENTS

Scripture quotations are from the
American Standard Version of the Bible
(1901), unless otherwise indicated.

PART ONE

THE RIGHTEOUSNESS OF GOD

1 The Righteousness of God

But now apart from the law a righteousness of God hath been manifested, being witnessed by the law and the prophets; even the righteousness of God through faith in Jesus Christ unto all them that believe; for there is no distinction; for all have sinned, and fall short of the glory of God; being justified freely by his grace through the redemption that is in Christ Jesus: whom God set forth to be a propitiation, through faith, in his blood, to show his righteousness because of the passing over of the sins done aforetime, in the forbearance of God; for the showing, I say, of his righteousness at this present season: that he might himself be just, and the justifier of him that hath faith in Jesus. Where then is the glorying? It is excluded. By what manner of law? of works? Nay: but by a law of faith. We reckon therefore that a man is justified by faith apart from the works of the law. . . . Do we then make the law of none effect through faith? God forbid: nay, we establish the law. (Rom. 3.21–28, 31)

Each time we recall how we were saved we are reminded of the love of God. But we should also remember something else—that it was not easy for God to provide salvation for us. Why? Because God has His nature and His way just as we humans have our nature and our way. Man's way is his method or habit of doing things; and it is closely related to his nature. God too has His own way—His definite method or procedure or rule of doing things. This is called the way of God. The Bible shows us that glory is God himself, holiness is His nature, and righteousness is His way.

The righteousness of God is His method of working. God's way of working reveals Him in the same way as a person may be known by the way he works. For example, a certain individual may have a very thorough way of doing things; his procedure is always highly exact. Whenever a matter is entrusted to him you know it will not be done carelessly but will be accomplished neatly and well. Since each person has his characteristic way of working, that person can easily be identified, for others will not do it in the same manner. Now this is also true of God. All His works bear a special mark which distinguish them as being of God. His way is related to himself, that is, to His nature. And His way is righteousness, for He cannot do anything unrighteous. He must satisfy His sense of righteousness in all His undertakings.

God's Salvation Must Meet God's Righteousness

For this reason, it poses a problem to God as to how to save us. On the one hand He does wish to save us; but on the other hand He cannot undertake anything against His nature. Were He to do so, He would become increasingly unhappy and uncomfortable. God can never do anything which infringes on His nature. Yet, without doubt, God is love. He knows how pitiful man is and how he needs to be saved. But God can only do this work in a way which satisfies His own heart. He will save us, yet without violating His own way.

Is God satisfied with the salvation which He has provided for us today? Thank God, His heart *is* satisfied. This salvation seems right in the eyes of God. Men, of course, are quite happy with the grace they have received. But God, when He gives us grace, must also be happy with himself. He cannot sigh and reluctantly say, "This is not what I would like to do, but for the sake of saving these souls I have to do it this way." No, God has His nature and His way. He must work till He himself is satisfied. He must be able to declare: "It is good." We know that in creating the earth and the heaven God pronounced "good" over everything He made except in the case of the firmament on the second day. (There is a reason behind this exception—but which we will not delve into at present.) If anything is not good, it cannot be reckoned as of God's doing. In all His workings, God keeps to His special procedure. His way is always perfectly righteous. He has no delight in anything unrighteous.

Being a righteous God, it is easier for Him to condemn our sin than it is to forgive us. Let me illustrate. A righteous man quite easily judges, according to righteousness, any sin he observes in other people. But it is not that easy for him to forgive. And so is it with God: for Him, whoever sins must perish. This action will fully manifest God's nature and vindicate His righteousness. But for God to forgive a sinner would hardly demonstrate His nature and righteousness. If one should appear before God and answer affirmatively that he has sinned, then his condemnation is justified. But if God were freely to forgive his sin, this would not be just for Him to do. For if God were to do this, He would be denying himself.

Let us remember that when God was preparing salvation for us, He seemingly was confronted with a most difficult problem. On the one hand He desired to forgive our sins, while on the other hand He must work in accordance with His own nature. Here was quite a dilemma. If God needed not to act according to righteousness, He could quickly forgive us. Contrariwise, though, it would be simple if He did not forgive our sins and condemned us to perish. Either of these two alternatives would be easy for God to choose. But He took neither of them. Here then is the quandary: we have sinned; we therefore should perish; God, though, wants to save us; yet He cannot be unrighteous.

These are the four factors that combined to create an enigma before God. God wishes to save us, but He cannot relax His righteousness. He desires to save us, yet He must work righteously. On the one hand He wants to be merciful to us, on the other hand He has to judge our sins. On the one side He wills to save us; on the other side He wishes to maintain righteousness. To use human terms, God here is the Executor as well as the Legislator. Can we imagine how He—being a Legislator and Executor—could save us without compromising righteousness? There is therefore a prior requirement which God must meet in His preparing salvation for us; namely, how to work out a salvation which suits His own righteousness. He has to show us that His forgiving us is perfectly just and is not a matter of overlooking sin.

The Lawfulness of Forgiveness

God, then, has to propound a way by which He can forgive us and at the same time satisfy His own righteousness. He must be able to keep His law as He forgives us. This is called the grace of God. God's grace means that all the laws of God are still kept in tact and yet we may be saved. Salvation implies that men can be saved while simultaneously God remains righteous. We know that God will not only save us but will also save us righteously. He cannot do a work which is subject to criticism. He is not willing to have men saved that they then may criticize Him as having performed unrighteously. Not at all; God always works justly. In saving us, He saves most righteously. He leaves no ground for any to criticize. He leaves us speechless. Furthermore, He must save us in such a way that the devil's mouth too is shut. He cannot save us in such a way that the devil may accuse Him as being unrighteous. No, He cannot do that. He will so save that neither man nor the devil has anything to say against Him. And lastly, He must save us to the extent that He himself has no more to say. The salvation of God must not only look right in the eyes of men and of the adversary but in His own sight as well. For God to save us is not at all difficult, but to save *justly* is quite another matter. The Bible affirms that in saving men God has so worked that neither the saved nor the unsaved, neither the devil nor even God himself has any complaint. This is called salvation. Salvation is God saving people with His righteousness; and this is God's masterpiece.

We all know that we are saved by grace. We need to know, however, that God's grace is governed by His righteousness. It may be said that the grace of God flows through the channel of God's righteousness. Truly, men need to be saved because all have sinned. But sin deserves punishment, and God cannot thoughtlessly forgive men's sin. When a criminal is apprehended and sent to the court, can the judge say, "Because his mother is advanced in age I will let him go" or, "Since he has three children in his family I will set him free"? If the judge should thus pronounce, and though his heart be right, his act is unrighteous. It is not justifiable to use unjust means to do a good deed. God will only do good justly. It is true that we need God to forgive us our sins, but He cannot do anything unjustly. God must find a way to keep himself from unrighteousness as well as to benefit us.

Our God cannot be unjust in anything, and certainly not in this matter of salvation. He must save us with righteousness.

How, then, does God accomplish a righteous salvation? He uses the cross. If it were not for the necessity of righteousness, the cross must certainly be termed a clumsy method. Why not just forgive outrightly? Why use the cross? Hence if righteousness were not involved, there would be no need for the cross. But God is the God of righteousness; and therefore the cross is indispensable. In view of our sin and its judgment, and in view of His own need to satisfy the demand of the law, God uses the cross to save us. The cross is the price which God pays for us.

Twenty years ago a preacher preached the gospel to a group of girl students. He spoke on the righteousness of God. He mentioned how God loves us and delights to forgive and save us, but that His salvation needs to be perfectly righteous. People have sinned, and they therefore must be repaid in punishment. God, however, uses the cross to repay His Law so that He can justly save us. The majority of the students did not understand this word. So the preacher used a parable. On the desk was a large vase. He turned to the principal of the school and asked, "If anyone damages any public property in your school, what should be done?" The lady principal answered, "It must be reimbursed." "Suppose this vase is worth five dollars, and a student smashes it to pieces. Will the school demand reparation?" asked the preacher. "According to the regulations of the school," replied the principal, "restitution must be made. If a person breaks the vase and gets by without paying for the damage, someone else may break a window later on and use this first case as a precedent for not making reparation. Then the regulations of the school would become obsolete." In other words, both the principal and the students had the responsibility of keeping the school regulations. It was the responsibility of the principal not to let the students damage school property. It was also her responsibility to demand reparation if school property were damaged. The student who broke the vase must pay for the damage according to the school regulations. If the student were financially unable to repay, what should the principal do? Should she insist on the reparation which the student could not possibly pay or should she drop the demand and herself become unrighteous? If it turned out that the principal had mercy on the student and wished to forgive her but at the same time had to be just and enforce the regulations of the school, there was but one thing the principal could do: she could take five dollars out of her own money and give it to the student, saying, "You have broken the vase, you must pay for the damage. Use this money as payment." According to righteousness, whoever damaged school property must pay for the damage; in this parable the money was paid, so the demand of the school regulations was satisfied. According to love, the principal was willing to give her own money to the student for payment; and thus the love of the principal was fully manifested.

This, therefore, is the meaning of the cross. God's

righteousness demands that whoever sins must be punished. We are like the student who sinned and was unable to pay back. God cannot be unrighteous and freely let us go. So, He provides the cross, which we sinners, and not God's Son, deserve to bear. All who come to God by the cross may then be justly saved, even as that student could be justly forgiven.

Our God, though desirous of saving us, cannot be unrighteous. He therefore gave us His Son that He might die for us on the cross. We have sinned, and hence we should be punished; but we have the cross to present to God. Before God granted us the cross, we would have had nothing to say if He had decided to punish us. But since He has given us the cross, He cannot but forgive our sins and accept us. Let us remember that upon our once having the cross, our salvation is based on the righteousness of God. *Without* the cross none can be saved, since God cannot be unrighteous. But *with* the cross, God has no way *not* to save us, because we are saved justly. The Lord Jesus has taken our punishment; therefore, the forgiveness of our sins is perfectly righteous. God cannot thoughtlessly forgive us; He forgives in accordance with His righteous procedure.

Boldly Come to God

Whether one can be a good Christian depends very largely on whether he understands the righteousness of God. Many Christians there are who are not clear on this point. They think their sins are forgiven purely because God has mercy on them. God is aware of how helpless they are, and hence He forgives them. What they do not know is that it is also the righteousness of God which effects their forgiveness. Due to lack of this knowledge, there are many who at times feel God *has* forgiven them and at other times do not feel that way. Let us ever be mindful that God *has* already given to us His Son who *has* paid the penalty of sin for us. Before He gave Jesus of Nazareth to us God was free to forgive or not to forgive. But having given Jesus of Nazareth to us, God is bound to forgive all who come to Him through Christ Jesus. Hallelujah! God *has* to forgive all who come to Him through Christ Jesus. He must forgive whether He is happy to forgive or not. Hallelujah! Today we come to God not only because of His love but also because of His righteousness.

Keep well in mind, then, the significance of righteousness. Righteousness gives us boldness before God. We look not to whether God is happy to forgive nor to how we feel, but we depend on the unchangeable righteousness of God. God has given Christ Jesus to us and now we approach Him through the Lord Jesus. He cannot help but forgive us. Before Jesus of Nazareth died, God could be thought to be free to forgive or not to forgive as He pleased. But since Jesus of Nazareth has died for us, God *must* forgive all who come through Christ Jesus. We come to God on the ground of righteousness.

Let me relate another story. There was once a Sunday School teacher who asked two little sisters how they were saved. The older sister stood up and said, "Thank God, I am saved by the grace of God." The younger sister stood up after her, saying, "Thank God, I am saved by the righteousness of God." The older sister touched her younger sister with her elbow, saying, "No, say that I am saved by the grace of God." The younger one, however, was very familiar with the Bible. So she recited a Scripture verse: "If we confess our sins, he is faithful and righteous to forgive us our sins, and to cleanse us from all unrighteousness" (1 John 1.9). The word of God tells us that our sins are forgiven and our unrighteousnesses are cleansed because of the righteousness of God. This little sister's testimony was very bold indeed.

We may say that anyone who really knows God does not tremble to come to Him. Can it be imagined that Noah trembled in the ark, fearful lest the ark should sink to the bottom of the water? Or that the firstborn of an Israelite trembled in the house splashed with blood for fear that the angel might mistakenly slay him? Remember, God has not carelessly forgiven us; He has instead forgiven us righteously. Such forgiveness is in line with His own nature. This forgiveness of His is so perfectly righteous that neither man nor the devil nor even God himself has any rebuttal to offer against it. Let us therefore rejoice and be glad before God. Let us rest in this confidence; and then we shall not be afraid. All who come to God through the cross have been delivered from condemnation and from judgment. Whenever we think of salvation and of righteousness, we can instantly burst into praise. We will praise God, for He has justly saved us!

Thank God, we are saved by His righteousness. We receive forgiveness through His righteousness. We have no fear when we come to Him through the Lord Jesus. We remember how God's righteousness has saved us and how His righteousness has made Him accept us. Hence let us say: "God, I thank You, I praise You. For the sake of the Lord Jesus, You cannot but accept me. If You had not given the Lord Jesus to me, I could only stand outside the door and beg of You. Now that You have given the Lord Jesus to me, I demand to enter in." God has given the Lord Jesus to us. Hallelujah! He now belongs to us! For this reason the Bible says: "Having therefore, brethren, boldness to enter into the holy place by the blood of Jesus" (Heb. 10.19). Any sign of doubt is wrong. Let all who have received the Lord Jesus say: "God, I thank You and I praise You, for You are righteous, and Your righteousness causes me to be forgiven."

2 Christ Our Righteousness

But of (God) are ye in Christ Jesus, who was made unto us wisdom from God, and righteousness and sanctification, and redemption. (1 Cor. 1.30)

To the praise of the glory of his grace, which he freely bestowed on us in the Beloved. (Eph. 1.6)

We have already discussed how righteous God is in saving us; we will now consider how He has made Christ our righteousness. Righteousness is especially related to God. If we are ever to come before Him, we must pay attention to this matter of righteousness. Without it, no one dare face God. We will recall that after they fell, Adam and Eve hid themselves among the trees of the garden when they heard the voice of God. They hid from the face of the Lord God, for they were both naked. By the mere hearing of His voice they were immediately aware of their own nakedness. Being uncovered, they could not see God. Here we understand that the Bible uses clothing to represent righteousness. If we are clothed with righteousness like a robe, we are then able to see God.

We have already been baptized unto Christ; yet there is one thing we should ask, which is, that since we now belong to Christ how can we daily appear before God? On what ground can we come to Him? What do we wear when we come? Without any doubt our sins have been cleansed and forgiven, but we still need to be clothed. Righteousness is not only something negative relating to sin and forgiveness; it is also something positive in bringing us into the presence of God. To appear before Him the issue of righteousness must be solved.

Surely we pray after we become Christians. But are there not times when we doubt if God really hears us? Why do we sometimes doubt this? It is because we feel we are not right, that we have many shortcomings which are all exposed to God. We do not think of this when we are not praying; but as soon as we commence to pray, we must settle the question of how we can come to God. This is something truly marvelous. We must be clothed with something in order to approach Him with boldness. This is the problem of righteousness, that of what we wear as we draw nigh to God.

On what ground do we appear before God? What do we have for Him to see and with which to be satisfied? God cannot accept us by overlooking our faults. He has to scrutinize us till He himself is well-pleased. Each time we come to Him we need righteousness.

When we stand before Him we must show Him righteousness. Whether we are bold or timid, strong or weak, rests on whether or not we have righteousness to show God. If we do not have righteousness we are afraid to be seen, because He will quickly detect our loopholes. If we have not righteousness, all our boldness will disappear and we will feel withered inside. But if we have righteousness, if we are so righteous that even God cannot complain, then we can be bold in approaching Him and can dare to pray to Him. We need to remember that one of the basic conditions for prayer is boldness. How can we pray without this holy confidence? How can we approach God unless we have boldness within us? What is boldness? It is that we may stand before God and be found blameless. This will give us confidence in prayer and strengthen our Christian life.

Our Own Righteousness

Now the question is: By what righteousness can we approach God? What kind is acceptable to Him? First of all, let us be clear that the righteousness we mention here is different from that in the first chapter. Earlier we spoke of the relationship between righteousness and sin, between the righteousness of God and our sin. Here, though, we speak of how we come into the presence of God, and what we bring to fully satisfy Him.

The difficulty with many people is probably right at this point: yesterday I prayed to God with great boldness. Why? Because yesterday I preached the gospel twice, and I read five chapters of the Bible; consequently I felt quite spirited before the Lord. Our courage is increased when we feel we are all right, good, and righteous. But our "righteousness" is a little bit strange. It is like a fever which sometimes runs high and sometimes runs low. Yesterday it seemed to be high, but today it cools down. Yesterday there was much interest in reading the Bible; today there is hardly any understanding. Yesterday I preached the gospel with zeal; today I have no desire to witness, so I cease after a few incoherent words. What is the consequence? I am not as ardent in prayer today as I was yesterday. As I approach God, I am quite sure that I will not be heard because I have not read the Bible well, witnessed well, lived well, or felt well. Do you see how our own righteousness is always up and down, hot and cold, good and bad, intermittently?

Our righteousness being of the up-and-down, hot-and-cold type, our Christian life will naturally follow suit. One day we have great boldness before God, the next day our boldness vanishes. One day we believe God hears our prayer, the following day we feel He has not heard us. Sometimes we stand without fear before God, sometimes we stand trembling. Our life is always one of vacillation. Why is it so? Because we come to God on the merit of our own conduct and our own righteousness. If our conduct is better, we feel stronger before God; but when our conduct is worse, our hearts grow colder. Thus our lives before God are like wind-blown candles—suddenly bright but then suddenly dark.

Christ Is Our Righteousness

What, then, *is* our righteousness? This is a basic lesson which we Christians must learn thoroughly. We ought to know that in providing for our salvation God solved the problem of righteousness as well as that of sin. Through righteousness God has forgiven our sins, and He has also prepared for us a righteousness by which we can always come to Him. Forgiveness is like taking a bath; righteousness is like wearing a robe. Among men we are clothed that we may appear before them. So too, God clothes us with righteousness that we may live before Him; that is, that we may see Him. He has already cleansed our sins and given us a righteousness by which we may live in His presence.

What is our righteousness? The word of God tells us that our righteousness is Christ—the Lord Jesus himself. "But of (God) are ye in Christ Jesus, who was made unto us wisdom from God, and righteousness and sanctification, and redemption" (1 Cor. 1.30). From this rich verse we will lift out but one item and concentrate our attention upon it alone—namely, that God has made Christ our righteousness.

Not the Righteousness of Christ

Before we discuss how Christ is our righteousness, we wish to explain briefly that the righteousness of Christ and Christ our righteousness are two totally distinct subjects. It is wrong to consider the righteousness of Christ as our righteousness. The righteousness of Christ cannot be our righteousness; it is Christ himself who is our righteousness.

The word found in 2 Peter 1.1—"the righteousness of our God and the Saviour Jesus Christ"—points to the righteousness which Christ himself possesses. If the Lord Jesus *himself* is not righteous, He is not qualified to be the Savior, and we have no way to be saved. This righteousness is purely for Christ himself, not for Him to give to us. The Bible never says the righteousness of the Lord Jesus saves us, because this righteousness is for the purpose of qualifying Him to be our Savior. His righteousness cannot be reckoned as our righteousness. His righteousness is that which He lives out while on earth. It is *His* personal standing before God. It is the righteousness of Christ's personal conduct. It has no way to be imparted to us. Christ's righteousness is what He himself has worked out. It is exclusively His and is absolutely unrelated to us. It is for this reason that the word of God never says we are "in Jesus". In being Jesus He is still the only begotten Son of God—He has not yet become the first-born Son and hence we are not yet the many sons. We therefore have no part in Him.

Let us understand that our union with Christ begins at His cross, not at His incarnation. Until the time of the cross, all that Christ has is exclusively His own; He has not yet shared anything with us. If a grain of wheat falls into the ground and dies, it bears much fruit (many grains). Only since the Lord Jesus has died are we now those fruits, those many grains. Our union with Christ begins at His death, not at His birth. *Calvary* is where we are united with Him; at Bethlehem there is no such union. Before Calvary, we can only view His righteousness; we cannot share in it. The Bible from its beginning to its end tells us that we are not saved by the righteousness of Christ nor do we become righteous by His righteousness. Our becoming righteous before God is only because of Christ himself.

Some may ask, Does not the Bible tell us that God has given us the righteous robe of the Lord Jesus? But we would counter, Does God's word say that God will clothe us with the righteous robe of the Lord Jesus or that He will clothe us with the Lord Jesus as a righteous robe? In other words, are we clothed with the righteousness of the Lord Jesus or clothed with the Lord Jesus himself? In point of fact, we have never read in God's word that we are clothed with the righteousness of the Lord Jesus; we read instead that we are clothed with the Lord Jesus: "Put ye on the Lord Jesus Christ" (Rom. 13.14).

We see here a most wonderful and distinctive thing: our righteousness before God is not the earthly conduct of the Lord Jesus, our righteousness before Him is the Lord Jesus, a living person. Today we come to God because we are clothed with the Lord Jesus himself. The Lord Jesus is our righteousness; and this is not the righteousness which He has, but He himself as righteousness. Accordingly, since the Lord Jesus lives forever, we have righteousness before God at all times. We may come to Him with boldness at any time, for we have the Lord Jesus as our righteousness.

Christ Is Righteousness

If our righteousness before God were our conduct we would be very unstable, because our conduct is sometimes good and sometimes bad; furthermore, our good conduct is always limited and can never meet the standard of God. Thank God, the righteousness we have before Him is not our conduct, but Christ; we are therefore immovable before Him. Today you may not be very strong and good. Satan will come and tempt you, saying, "What are you, after all? God will not have such a person as you." But you can reply: "You have forgotten, Satan, that my righteousness before God is not my good conduct of yesterday nor is it my less good conduct of today; but my righteousness before Him is Christ. Christ has not changed today, so my righteousness remains unchanged." Should the garment we wear be of our own making, it would be dirty rags and we would be quite unable to meet God. But we are today clothed with Christ; hence we have boldness to see God. Oh! This is deliverance, this is emancipation, this is the foundation of Christian doctrine.

Suppose we imagine ourselves asking a brother who knows the word of God: "Will your righteousness ever fail?" He will answer, "No, never." "But will your conduct ever fail?" we may ask. He will say, "Certainly." Do you see that his righteousness will never fail, though his conduct may? His righteousness is not his conduct. If this were true, then when his conduct failed, his righteousness would fail too. Yet his righteousness is not his conduct, it is not that which is subject to failure; his righteousness is the Christ who never fails. And so our righteousness too never fails; it is as unfailing as Christ is. Now this may sound too bold, but it is the word of God. Our righteousness is Christ. Because He never fails, our righteousness never fails either.

Some may perhaps inquire, Does it then mean that our bad conduct does not matter? It definitely does matter. For the Bible shows us that a Christian has *two* garments: one is the Lord Jesus, for He is our robe, He is our righteousness; the other is the bright and pure fine linen of Revelation 19.8: "For the fine linen is the righteous acts of the saints." ("Righteous acts" is "righteousnesses" in the original, meaning the many acts of righteousness.) All the good conduct of a Christian—all his outward righteousnesses—come from grace as a result of the working of the Holy Spirit in him; they are not something which he has naturally. As we approach God we are not naked, because we are clothed with Christ who is our righteousness. However, as we appear before the judgment seat of Christ we must bring our own righteousness, that which is called the righteousnesses of the saints (see 2 Cor. 5.10, 1 Cor. 4.5). This present chapter deals exclusively with Christ our righteousness, not with the righteousnesses of the saints.

There is one name in the Old Testament which is very precious. It is "Jehovah our righteousness" (Jer. 23.6, 33.16). Jehovah is our righteousness, therefore our righteousness is not our conduct. May God open our eyes that we may see the gospel, even the foundation of the gospel. As we come to God, Christ—not our conduct—is our righteousness. The Lord is our righteousness. We come to Him through Christ. What else is as firm and immovable as this?

Each time we approach God, we need to remember that Christ is our righteousness. If we see Him as this, we will stand in the presence of God with confidence. We will come as little children, saying to Him, "Look, I come today clothed with Christ." God looks and He finds no defect. The more He looks the better we look, for Christ is absolutely without blemish; He is perfect.

"His grace, which he freely bestowed on us in the Beloved" (Eph. 1.6). This verse includes the thought of our being accepted in the Beloved. Just as God accepts His beloved Son, even so He accepts us in the Beloved. We are accepted in the Beloved, and we are as accepted as the Beloved. God accepts us as He accepts His own Son. Whatever position the beloved Son has belongs to all who are in the Beloved. This is truly most glorious.

When Balak asked Balaam to curse God's people—the children of Israel—Balaam was forced to admit: God "hath not beheld iniquity in Jacob; neither hath he seen perverseness in Israel; Jehovah his God is with him, and the shout of a king is among them" (Num. 23.21). Even though he was a covetous prophet, he was not free to speak as he wished. God showed him what to say, and he had to prophesy according to God's wish.

But on the other hand, when the Israelites murmured against God after they had heard the evil report of the spies, God said to them: "Your dead bodies shall fall in this wilderness; and all that were numbered of you, according to your whole number, from twenty years old and upward, that have murmured against me, surely ye shall not come into the land, concerning which I sware that I would make you dwell therein, save Caleb the son of Jephunneh, and Joshua the son of Nun" (Num. 14.29–30). Let us remember that according to conduct, they had actually sinned; so have we sinned. Never fancy, after hearing these words of Balaam, that we are so good that we have no sin. God did not speak here of the good conduct of the Israelites; rather, He spoke of seeing a righteousness in Israel. It was through their offerings and the righteousness of the sacrifices that God did not behold iniquity in Jacob nor perverseness in Israel.

We know that the sacrifices represent or typify the Lord Jesus Christ. Because we are in Christ and are accepted in the Beloved, we may approach God with boldness. Our righteousness before Him is as perfect as Christ; since Christ is our righteousness, God cannot find any iniquity in us. Because we have received the Lord Jesus as our Savior, God looks on us as though we have never sinned. Hence do not be made timid by the remembrance of your past history, since we know He has already forgiven all our sins. Thank God, He has put us in Christ that we may stand before Him as though we had never sinned. Christ is our righteousness, and so God is able to declare that He has not perceived iniquity in Jacob nor has He seen sin in Israel. If we come to God through Christ, can we come in any other way than in boldness?

Losing boldness in coming to God is due to our looking at ourselves. Whenever we are afraid of seeing God we have not seen Christ. If we see Him—and not ourselves—we shall have confidence every time we approach God. Christ never fails, therefore we also fail not before God. Praise Him, our righteousness does not ebb and flow; it remains constant. Our conduct is subject to ups and downs, but our righteousness is not susceptible to change. Should some ask us if the conduct of a Christian, his zeal and love, is open to change, our answer would have to be yes. We would be deceiving ourselves if we were to deny such a possibility. Yet if the subject were our righteousness, we would say it is not subject to change for it is unchangeable. The word of God clearly declares that the unchanging Christ is our righteousness.

"Of (God) are ye in Christ Jesus, who was made unto us . . . righteousness" (1 Cor. 1.30). After the Lord was raised from the dead and was made Christ, God put us in Him who is our righteousness. We are clothed with Christ our righteousness. As Christ never changes before God, so we may come to Him daily with boldness.

May God open our eyes to see that we do not rely on our conduct or work either before or after we are saved. This does not mean that we can be careless in our conduct. We shall speak on this in the next chapter. Here we focus on the point of how we approach God. We come to Him by Christ, by Christ being our righteousness. Hence it is forever firm and immovable. Hallelujah, praise our Lord!

3 We Become the Righteousness of God

> Him who knew no sin he made to be sin on our behalf; that we might become the righteousness of God in Him. (2 Cor. 5.21)

We have already mentioned two matters: first, how God saves us with His own righteousness; and second, how Christ, with whom we are clothed as we approach God, is our righteousness. This means (1) that we are not saved by our righteousness but by the righteousness of God. God saves us not because we are righteous, but because He is righteous. He cannot be unrighteous towards us because He cannot deny himself. If we believe in Christ, God has to save us. It is absolutely impossible for Him not to save us.

And it means (2) that our righteousness before God is not our conduct but Christ. Our conduct and righteousness before Him are not the same; they should therefore not be confused as though our conduct is our righteousness before Him and vice versa. The word of God shows us that our conduct is subject to changes, but our righteousness before Him is forever stable because our righteousness is Christ. Thank God, one day He opened our eyes to see that our righteousness before Him is not our conduct, but Christ. This gives us release to pray and to commune with God with boldness.

We will now consider the third matter, which is found in 2 Corinthians 5.21: "Him who knew no sin he made to be sin on our behalf; that we might become the righteousness of God." We who sinned are saved because Christ was made sin for us. We who are saved through the work of Christ have now become the righteousness of God in Him. This is a direct complement to 1 Corinthians 1.30. There we see that "Christ became our righteousness"; here in 2 Corinthians we find that "we become the righteousness of God." Whoever acknowledges the One that was without sin and yet was made sin for us becomes himself the righteousness of God.

God's Redemption Reveals God's Righteousness

We do not know how to say it, for it is truly most wonderful: we become the righteousness of God! The Bible tells us that our righteousness is Christ and God's righteousness is we ourselves. God has made Christ our righteousness, He has also made us His righteousness in Christ. What does it mean by our becoming the righteousness of God? It means that if anyone wants to learn and to see the righteousness of God, he need only find a Christian, for it is expressed in the life of a Christian. For this reason, a Christian is the righteousness of God.

Before we believe in the Lord we are blind to God's standards for righteousness and unrighteousness. But even after we become Christians, we may still be confused in identifying what is righteous and what is unrighteous. God will therefore not only save us but also teach us the lesson on righteousness. In His redemption He not only saves the unrighteous but He also instructs us as to what righteousness is.

In the first chapter we noticed that God does not thoughtlessly forgive our sins; for sin is a violation of law, and God is a law-abiding One. He loves us, but He cannot violate His own law. He desires to forgive us, yet He must also keep His law. Because of this, He has paid the price for us. This is called redemption. In order to forgive us, He sends His Son to bear in His body the penalty which we deserve. Since Christ has borne our sins, we may come to God through Christ. All who approach Him through the Lord Jesus will not be rejected, for the cross of Christ has already satisfied the demand of God's righteousness.

Some people might think that if God wishes to save us why can He not save us right away? Why must He send His Son to the world? Why must He cause the Lord Jesus to die on the cross and have His blood shed? Why should He make such a big thing out of it? Such people have never thought of the involvement of righteousness in redemption. Of course

God is most anxious to forgive our sins, but in the process of doing so He cannot be unrighteous. His heart is for saving us, yet He must maintain His righteousness. What would be the effect if He were to lightly save us, and abolish hell, death, and the lake of fire? The effect would be tremendous, for in abolishing hell, death, and the lake of fire, He would at the same time be abrogating His righteousness. Though He is not responsible to anybody else, He is nonetheless responsible to himself. He must be righteous towards himself.

A Christian coming to God through Christ declares to the world that herein is the righteousness of God. It means that He has not forgiven the sin of men groundlessly or carelessly, but He has forgiven sin in a most righteous manner. God has given to us His Son who has satisfied the demand of His law for us. Consequently, as we stand before Him in Christ we become the righteousness of God. This refers not to a Christian's conduct but to his manifesting the righteousness of God through the redemption of Christ.

Learn to Be Righteous

Having come in by this way of righteousness, we are encouraged to learn a lesson; which is, that we Christians must learn to be righteous. We must not be loose in our daily walk. Since God has been so righteous in saving us, we must be righteous lest we stand as a contradiction to Him. Because of redemption, we as the saved manifest the righteousness of God; because of the teaching that is brought to us through redemption our lives must also manifest the righteousness of God.

We ought to live righteously. We should always remember that even in saving us God cannot be unrighteous. He cannot be unrighteous towards himself, for His nature is righteous and hence He cannot deny himself. Being the specimen of God's righteousness, how can we do anything unrighteous? Since the only one and true God needs to be righteous, ought we not to live justly on earth?

Let us quickly learn a lesson here: all who are unrighteous are not of God; all who take advantage of other people are a contradiction to God; and all who fail in their various duties are unlike God. For the sake of righteousness, God has paid the price of righteousness—the giving of His Son. It is for righteousness' sake that God has given His Son, Jesus of Nazareth, the crucified One. Truly, God has paid such a tremendous price for the sake of righteousness. Can we be unrighteous out of fear of paying the price? We may find it convenient and even advantageous for a fleeting moment, but we shall be unrighteous people and shall eventually eat the fruit of unrighteousness.

Let me say that when we first begin to walk in the Way, we should realize how we entered in. In saving us, God has not brought us in through the back door. No, He has opened the front gate and let us in there. Praise be to God, we are saved in the most open and just way. No one can complain, because He saves us according to righteousness. If there were any tint of unrighteousness to it, the devil would surely remonstrate, since he always stands in opposition to God. But we thank God that He has provided such a salvation that the mouth of the devil is forever sealed. He has saved us to such a degree that none is able to overturn it. God, says the apostle, "is faithful and righteous to forgive us our sins, and to cleanse us from all unrighteousness" (1 John 1.9). He saves us according to righteousness. And this is the way that we enter in. This being true, we cannot afford to be careless in anything in our lives.

Hence we must learn the principle of righteousness. What is righteousness? Righteousness means owing nothing to anybody: Take not what is undeserved and give not what is improper. Let us reinforce this by stating that as God cannot be unrighteous towards himself so we who belong to Him ought not to be unrighteous. We should not owe any man anything. Whether we are good Christians who are making good progress depends a great deal on our understanding of, and feeling towards, righteousness when we first entered upon the Way. Many so-called Christians cause plenty of heartache to others because they never seem to have any sense of righteousness, are not even aware of what unrighteousness is. Some, upon having become Christians, have never once apologized or made any restitution. Is it because everything they had done or now do is right? If we do not acknowledge our faults, there can be only two possible explanations: either we are always right and never wrong, or else we will not confess our fault. May God be merciful to us that we may not deceive ourselves into thinking we have never done wrong; that we may not refuse—due to hardness of heart or a desire to save face—to acknowledge our fault.

Deal with All Unrighteousness

In learning righteousness, we must learn to deal with all unrighteousnesses. Before we became Christians we probably committed many unrighteous acts—such as defrauding or cheating people, unknowingly taking possession of other people's things, and so forth.

Sometimes, though, people may not be unrighteous in material things, but they instead infringe upon the rights of others. Each person has his right, and if we do not give him the right which is his due, we commit an unrighteous act against him. Some parents frequently quarrel; they do not give their children their due of peaceful days; they encroach on the rights of the children. This is unrighteousness. Some husbands do not fulfill their duty as husbands, some wives do not perform their duty as wives—these are unrighteousnesses. We are now Christians; we therefore need to deal with these unrighteous matters. We need to keep in mind that whether we walk the course before us in good fashion or not depends on how well we learn this first lesson. The redemption of God teaches us that having been saved so righteously by God we ought to live righteously on earth. As soon as we learn of anything unrighteous in us, we must deal with it immediately. For all unrighteousnesses are sins.

Many Christians consider only such things as pride and jealousy, murder and robbery to be sins; they do not see what unrighteousness really is. But God will bring us to perceive, one after another, what it is. Whenever an unrighteousness is found, instant dealing is required. If we do not deal with it we will not be able to manifest the righteousness of God, nor will people see in us what the righteousness of God is. Consequently we must so live as to make known the righteousness of God.

We shall now attempt to explain more concretely how to deal with unrighteousness.

Deal with Unrighteous Money

What touches people most is money; accordingly, we must learn first of all to be righteous in monetary matters. We should not spend other people's money; we must not steal the money of others. We cannot use improper means to make others' money ours. What is gained through improper means, whether consciously or unconsciously, is unrighteous. We must deal with it. Furthermore, we must not borrow money and then not return it. When we first begin as Christians, we should try our best to clear up any monetary problem. As our attention is directed by God to any debt or fraud or extortion, we must deal faithfully with each case. If we have cheated the government in revenue and tax, we ought to make reparation.

We have to be clear on this subject of money. We must deal with the past as the Lord indicates it to us; thus will we keep ourselves pure in this in the future.

If we are careless in this area, we will be careless in everything. In case there is no strength to repay, we still need first to confess and then try our best to make restitution.

Deal with All Material Indebtedness

Besides money, we must also take care of all kinds of material indebtedness. We should not have the habit of delighting in using things which belong to other people nor should we borrow things without returning them to the owners. Oftentimes we have a bad habit of being careful in our own things but careless in things which belong to other people. This too is unrighteous. We must learn to be careful with other people's property. If the thing borrowed is still there, return it to the owner. If the thing is lost, buy one and return the same, or repay according to its cost. Certain things should not be borrowed again. We need to exercise great caution in these material things, for many have failed in this respect. We ought to manifest the righteousness of God in this area.

Deal with Greedy Habits

We must deal with our greedy heart as well as with things material. It is a bad habit to be greedy; we need to learn to seek the welfare of others and be considerate of others. We must not always think of taking advantage of other people, trying to get something out of them. Learn never to damage others in order to profit ourselves. It is unrighteous.

To use a small illustration, suppose a pedicab driver asks for an extremely low fare because he is not familiar with the distance of the destination. If we are righteous, can we take advantage of his ignorance? By all appearances, it cannot be reckoned as wrong if we give what he has asked for. But in accordance with the Christian standard, we should add some extra for him. We need to understand that greediness is as unrighteous as robbery. Even though people may agree to something out of helplessness, Christians ought not take advantage of such a situation. In our transactions with others, we must not count how much we are profited but how much is fair. Righteousness demands that the conscience of a Christian be satisfied. It is not what other people say but whether our conscience is at rest.

Deal with Any Encroachment on Others' Rights

Unrighteousness is not limited to material things; it can intrude upon the rights of other people. For example, as pertaining to a public place, there is a time for rest and relaxation as well as a time for work. Rest is the right of people. If during the time of their relaxation we shout and make great noise, we encroach on others' rights. This is unrighteous. It is also unrighteous to read other people's letters and documents without their permission, for this too is a violation of their rights. In getting on or off public transportation such as buses or trains, we should keep in line. It is unrighteous to step ahead from behind, because this trespasses the rights of other people. We ought to be sensitive to things such as these and handle them faithfully lest we be unrighteous.

Confess Our Fault

If we are willing to be enlightened by God, He will show us the many unrighteous acts we have committed. Then when we see our faults, let us not be afraid to confess them. At the beginning of our Christian life faults are inevitable; what we should fear most, however, is not knowing our faults, or knowing them but without confessing them. Not knowing our faults reveals that we are in darkness. Our sins can be forgiven, but darkness is unforgivable. If we confess our sins, the Lord will forgive us; but darkness keeps us from knowing our sins, which in turn keeps us from receiving forgiveness. The Lord says to us, "I am the light of the world: he that followeth me shall not walk in the darkness, but shall have the light of life" (John 8.12). Without light, how can we distinguish black from white? If we are in the light, we shall be able to see what is unrighteous, what is sin.

To a new believer, nothing is more essential than to know what unrighteousness is. It is exceedingly important for a Christian to increase in his identification of, and his dealings with, all unrighteousnesses.

A brother once testified: "After I was saved, the first year I wrote over one hundred letters to people to confess my sins. I sent out about the same amount of letters of confession in the second year. Even so, I knew only sin but not unrighteousness. I only knew that I had cheated people, I had slandered people, I had treated others with cunning. These were sins, so I dealt with them. However, I still had not seen what unrighteousness was. I did not understand what was encroachment on other people's rights. I had yet to see that I must render to all their due.

"Three years after I was saved, I read a story in a magazine. It ran like this: There was a Christian convention at a certain place. It was raining that day. One man who sat in the front row put his raincoat on the back of his chair. When a speaker made his way to the platform, he unknowingly touched the raincoat so that one of its sleeves dropped to the ground. The speaker was not conscious of it, so he in his muddy shoes stepped on the sleeve. Immediately he was aware of it, but he merely kicked it aside and went on. He spoke well and he was very familiar with the Bible. But the narrator of the story commented that he did not care how well the man spoke. He was only interested to see how the speaker would deal with the sleeve of the raincoat after he descended from the platform. Well, the speaker came down from the platform; he again kicked aside the sleeve of the raincoat and went to his seat. So the narrator concluded with these words—'This was unrighteousness.'

"I never before knew what was unrighteousness, but I saw it that day as I read the story. The word unrighteousness seemed to loom large before me. What is it? Unrighteousness is trampling on other people. The speaker should not have kicked the other person's raincoat aside and sat down. He should have at least apologized to the owner or, better yet, have had it cleaned. What he did was unrighteous."

We need to know what unrighteousness is. Unrighteousness is overstepping one's boundary, treading on other people and causing them to suffer loss. Since God has made us His righteousness, we are made to manifest the righteousness of God so that when others see us they see His righteousness. How then can we be unrighteous in our daily lives?

Pray and Encourage One Another

Finally, let us mention this: that we ourselves must be righteous. If we notice unrighteousness in other people, we should pray for them. The problem often, though, is this, that when we are righteous, we tend to be fretful and angry at seeing others' unrighteousness. We do not want to have anything to do with them; we are not even willing to say hello to them. Such an attitude is totally ineffectual, for they need light just as we do.

We did not know our fault during the time when we saw not. We may have just seen it since yesterday. If our brothers or sisters have unrighteousness, how can we not be concerned? We cannot ignore them or reject them. We must pray for them, asking God to enlighten them that they too may see. We need to learn how to pray for other people. We need to learn how to speak the truth in love.

Meanwhile, we must deal quite strictly with ourselves. Remember, that as the righteousness of God in the world today we must manifest in our lives how righteous our God is, so that people may give glory and praise to Him. Let us ask Him to make us a righteous people. Seeing that the salvation of God is righteous, let us ask God to enable us to manifest His righteousness in all things.

PART TWO

CHRIST IS MADE OUR WISDOM

1 Christ Is Made Our Wisdom

But of [God] are ye in Christ Jesus, who was made unto us wisdom from God, both righteousness and sanctification and redemption. (1Cor. 1.30 mg.)

In the Bible we find there are various ways of presenting Christ as our life. What does Christ our life really mean? It is not as simple as we usually think. 1 Corinthians 1.30 explains the meaning of Christ made our life, and this verse can be divided into two parts: (1) "Of God are ye in Christ Jesus"—which speaks of our relationship with Christ; and (2) "Who was made unto us wisdom from God"—which denotes Christ's relationship to us. In other words, one part tells us how we are in Christ, the other shows us how Christ is in us. We must notice these two sides. As regards an understanding of these two, some Christians emphasize the first part while others emphasize the second. Regardless to which side we tend, any imbalance will cause problems to our Christian living. We therefore need to have knowledge of both—knowing how we are in Christ and how Christ is in us.

God gives the Lord Jesus to us not for the sake of making Him our teacher that we may imitate His example, but for the purpose of causing us to have Him as our life so that His life may be manifested through us. If we do not have the life of Christ we are not Christians at all; yet if, having His life, we do not realize how He is our life, our Christian walk will not be satisfactory and we will fail to manifest the life of Christ. How, then, can we have Christ as our life? This is most foundational.

The Lord Jesus is a man as well as God. How can we have Him to be our life? It seems to be an impossible thing. There is no way for us to solve this predicament; God alone can solve it for us. Although with man this is impossible, with God all things are possible. We are therefore told in 1 Corinthians 1.30 that this thing is done wholly by God. Had God not done it, then for Christ to be our life would be an absolute impossibility. Hence the first part of this scripture says that "of God are ye in Christ Jesus"; this first half of the work is performed by God. The latter segment of the same verse continues by stating that Christ "was made unto us wisdom from God"; so that this second half of the work is likewise wrought by God. It is not we who are able to make the Lord Jesus our wisdom, rather is it God who makes Him our wisdom. Consequently, this matter of Christ being our life is entirely accomplished by God. Whether it is the first part or the second part, nothing can be accomplished without Him. It is unquestionably God who has made Christ our wisdom.

Of God Are We in Christ

In order to make Christ our life, where does God commence His work? He does not first put the life of Christ in us, instead He first puts us in Christ. Before He can put Christ in us He needs to put us in Christ. The first thing He will do is to establish our relationship with Christ. Unless we have a relationship with the Lord we are in no position to have Him in us as our life. We must first be in Christ, and then we can have Him in us. This is the order by which God works.

Why does God want to place us in Christ? Because we are all sinners, and possessors of the life of Adam. Before God is able to give us a new life, He has to deal with us sinners, who are the progeny of Adam's life. And this dealing He cannot apply directly upon us, for were He to do this we would all die and cease to live. Were He to deal directly with our sins, we would have no alternative to eternal death.

God has to deal with our Adamic life as well as with our sins on the one hand, and yet not bring us to death on the other hand. How does He solve this dilemma? He exercises His power to put us in Christ, so that when He deals with Christ He at the same time deals with us. We are all included in Christ; consequently, whatever God has done to Christ is also done to us. The effect of His dealing with Christ is the same as though we ourselves had been dealt with. Such is the basic teaching of the Bible concerning the Lord Jesus our Savior.

What judgment did God forewarn Adam of in the Garden of Eden if the latter should violate God's command and eat the fruit of the tree of the knowledge of good and evil? He announced: "In the day that thou eatest thereof thou shalt surely die." To eat the forbidden fruit was to sin, and in the day of sinning there would come in death: for death is the penalty of sin. If man sins, he must be punished. He who sins must die. Now it is best for man not to sin. Nevertheless sin has already been committed, and death has become a certainty. As sin is a fact which cannot be denied, so death as the natural consequence of sinning cannot be revoked.

What shall be done? God must on the one hand deliver us to death completely and must on the other hand cause us to live: this will be salvation. Thank God, He has appointed a way of salvation, and that is by sending a Savior to come and die for us. In view of this, Christ must be born. If He is not born, He cannot die for us. Without the flesh, how can He die? Hence Christ is born to become flesh in order that He may die in our stead. In His death He bears our penalty, in His death He becomes our salvation. How can Christ die for us? By God putting us in Him. This constitutes a key teaching of the entire Bible. We do not know nor are we able to comprehend how God exercises His authority and power to put us in Christ, but we do know that 1 Corinthians 1.30 clearly informs us that "of God are ye in Christ." And "of God" means that this is done by God.

What is meant by our being in Christ? Perhaps an illustration here can help to explain it. In China there are lacquer cases. These cases form a unit, one after another being enclosed within the other. Outwardly speaking there seems to be only one case, but in opening it there are a number of them. A big case includes in it quite a few smaller cases. So are we in Christ. "To be in Christ" is in direct contrast to "to be in Adam". We all are descendants of Adam, we all being in him. Adam is like the big lacquer case, and we are like the many smaller cases inside. From this large case there emerges many small cases, so that from Adam comes forth so many of us. We see many by taking out the many from the one; we see one if we put the many back into the one. Viewing the matter from our side, we are many individuals; but viewing from God's side, we in Adam are one man. Like the many small cases within one big case, they all appear to be one. Because we all are in Adam, therefore "through the one man's disobedience [i.e., Adam's] the many were made sinners." Since we are one in Adam, we are all condemned. Now according to the very same principle God comes to rescue us. He puts us all in Christ; and "even so through the obedience of the one [Christ] shall the many be made righteous." Due to the fact that we are one in Christ, all of us come to "justification of life" (see Rom. 5.18,19). Just as God sees so many of us as one in Adam, even so does He see us as one in Christ. Adam is like the first big lacquer case, and Christ is like a second big lacquer case. And even as we are one in the first big case (Adam) so we are one in the second big case (Christ). Hence the Bible calls the Lord Jesus "the second man" and "the last Adam" (1 Cor. 15.45–47). The Lord Jesus is the last Adam, for God has included all of us in Him.

When Jesus of Nazareth lives on earth as man, He is one person; but when He ascends to the cross, God puts us all in Him.* Therefore, when Jesus of Nazareth is crucified, the cross is not only *His* personal cross but is also *our* cross. Since God has put us in Christ, all who are in Him naturally share His cross.** We must know indeed that the cross of Christ is also our cross. If God has not put us in Christ, we

---

*It needs to be noted parenthetically, though, that speaking in terms of the glorious life of the Lord, even before the foundation of the world God has chosen us in Christ (Eph. 1.4). At that time there is no connection with sin. The life is Christ himself. Through death on the cross and resurrection this life is given to all who believe in Him, thus establishing a subjective relationship between the believers and Christ. Speaking in terms of the solution of the problem of the old creation, however, God puts us in Christ when He is crucified on the cross (Rom. 6.3-6), and thus are we united with Him. During that time, it is by now related to sin, which, though, is taken away by the death of Christ. Consequently, the death and resurrection of the Lord accomplish two things: one is the solving of the problem of sin and the old man that Adam passes on to us, and the other is the giving to us by God the eternal life which exists before the world's foundation. This present message deals only with the "in Christ" of Romans 6; it does not touch upon the "in Christ" before the foundation of the world.—*Author*

**This speaks only of the effect of the cross, not in any sense the sharing of Christ's vicarious death.—*Translator*

have no relationship with the cross; but being put in Him by God, we have a definite relationship to the cross. At the moment Christ is crucified we are all included in Him. Being included in Him, His experience of the cross is also our experience. Hence Romans 6.6 declares that "our old man was crucified with him."

Were we not in Christ, we would not be able to be crucified with Him. No wonder someone has observed: If not *in* the Lord, then not *with* the Lord. How spiritual and scriptural is this word. Let us remember that if we wish to be with Christ, we have to be in Him. How can we be with the Lord if we are not first in the Lord? This concerns our basic faith about which we must be very clear.

"Of God are ye in Christ Jesus"—this is something entirely done by God. Because we do not know this fact, the church needs to preach the gospel to make it known. The church is to proclaim this heaven- and earth-shaking fact to all men, telling them that God has already included mankind in Christ—so that when the Lord Jesus was crucified, God in judging Him has also judged all who are in Him. Judgment is now past. And this is the gospel. The gospel is what God has done for us in Christ. The gospel is: that God has included us in Christ, so that when He deals with Him He deals also with us. In Christ we have been dealt with, and God has completely solved our problem of man as well as our problem of sin. In short, we have died in Christ. Wherefore Romans 6.11 declares: "Even so reckon ye also yourselves to be dead unto sin, but alive unto God in Christ Jesus."

We have died in Christ Jesus. Upon hearing this fact what should we do? We are human beings, we have our will. If we believe in this fact, we should express ourselves in some concrete way. Now this is why we are baptized after we believe in the Lord and are saved. What is the meaning of baptism? It is to be baptized into Christ Jesus, even baptized into His death (Rom. 6.3,4). In other words, since God has put us in Christ we should so act as to show people how we are in Him. When in baptism we are submerged in the water, do we get buried in the water but rise no more? No. We rise up very quickly. So that in coming out of the water we express our being raised with Christ from the dead. Whoever comes up out of the water is a resurrected person. Therefore, when we are baptized we act out what God has accomplished in Christ for us. It is spiritual performance.

At the moment Christ is on the cross God puts us in Him and concludes this man of Adam. He must deal with this Adam; the account has to be settled. Just as we were born originally in Adam, so is it only through death that we are delivered from Adam. By being baptized into the death of Christ we are henceforth finished and are liberated from Adam. This is the first part of God's work. With regard to the second part—that is, Christ in us—we must go once more to 1 Corinthians 1.30, which in its latter segment states that Christ "was made unto us wisdom from God."

Christ Is Made unto Us Wisdom from God

Having dwelt on the fact of our being in Christ, we will now focus on the matter of Christ in us. How does it come about that Christ is in us? Christ *in us* hinges on resurrection. Because the Lord Jesus has been resurrected and dwells in the Holy Spirit—for He is not only a man but also a man in the Spirit—therefore, He is in us. The Lord Jesus has said, "My flesh is meat indeed, and my blood is drink indeed" (John 6.53–56). But only as a man in the Spirit may He be received into us. Had He remained as He formerly was on earth, He could not be taken in by us.

Let us realize that we eat the *fruit* of the tree of life, not the tree of life. A tree we can neither feed on nor take in. When the Lord Jesus was a man on earth He could be likened to the tree of life. Those who lived on earth at that time had no way to receive Him into themselves, just as today we cannot receive anyone into ourselves. If Jesus had not become the risen Lord but had simply continued on earth as before, He would forever be He, and we would forever be we, since there is absolutely no way to take Him in. Jesus of Nazareth, however holy and lovely He is, cannot be received into ourselves because He is a man. But today He not only is a man, He also has been raised from the dead and is now in the Spirit. Thus has He become the Lord who is receivable by us.

The Holy Spirit, it should be noted, is actually the Lord coming in another form (see John 14.16–20). Hence His name is also called "the Spirit of Jesus" (Acts 16.7) or "the Spirit of Christ" (Rom. 8.9). After the Lord Jesus is clothed with the Holy Spirit Christ becomes the Lord who can be received into us. Otherwise we would never be able to enjoy Him. In resurrection Christ is clothed with the Holy Spirit. When we receive the Holy Spirit we receive Christ, just as in receiving the Son we receive the Father. Just as in former days people seeing the Son also saw the Father, so now, as we know the Holy Spirit we likewise know the Son. The Lord Jesus is risen, He is clothed with the Holy Spirit; we may therefore receive Him into us, taking Him as our life. Whoever accepts the Lord Jesus, and no matter how clear or unclear he is, is given this experience by God.

God puts us in Christ—this is the first thing; He then makes Christ our wisdom—this is the second thing. These two actions are not accomplished by us. We cannot by ourselves enter into Christ or cause Christ to come into us. God alone can do both.

What is meant by "Christ is made our wisdom"? Let us at the outset more accurately re-punctuate the second part of 1 Corinthians 1.30. In accordance with the original text, a colon may rightly be placed after "wisdom from God"—thereby conveying the thought that wisdom includes the three things which follow: namely, righteousness and sanctification and redemption. Chapters 1–3 of 1 Corinthians deal persistently with God's wisdom versus man's wisdom. We accordingly consider wisdom to be the general topic, while righteousness and sanctification and redemption can be viewed as explaining how Christ is made our wisdom.

In order to understand what is meant by "Christ is made our wisdom", we must first be clear what life is. When, for example, temptation comes to stir you up, you know you should be patient. But whence does your patience originate? It may be said that what supplies you with patience is actually your life. You need to exercise your life to be patient. Apart from your life you are dead, you cannot be patient. You need to mobilize your life to supply yourself with patience. Or, you feel you should not be slothful but diligent. To be diligent your life has to supply you with it. Or, when someone is in trouble, you know you should show love and be helpful. But where does your love come from? It is your life that causes you to love. For this reason, whenever we are faced with something, the first reaction which is produced within us is the manifestation of our life. All these reactions flow out from our life. What precipitates these reactions is life. Without it there can be no reactions of this kind. Life produces these reactions. We face situations all the time, and we react all the time. We exercise our life to meet outside demands on all occasions; there is not an instance when we do not use our life.

Now God gives Christ to us that He may be our life as well as our substitute on the cross. Previously we reacted to all outside demands with our own life. If our own life was adequate, we did well; if inadequate, we did not do so well; and if totally incompetent, we simply failed. We always used our own life to react to and to manage all affairs. But today God has given Christ to us, and He wants Him to be our life. Before we received the Lord Jesus, we lived by ourselves; but after we receive Him, God purposes to let Him live for us. Since the Lord Jesus Christ dwells in us to be our life, we need no more to depend on our former life to live. Not that the Lord Jesus gives us so many commandments, shows us so many ideas, and tells us so many doctrines for us to comply with; but that He himself is in us as our life to do everything for us. Hereafter we should live by the life of the Lord Jesus. Formerly we reacted to all outside demands with our own life, hereafter we ought to let the life of Christ take over.

Knowing what Christ our life means, we can now proceed to explain how God makes Christ our wisdom. Now you have been a Christain for a long time. Aside from your own wisdom have you ever experienced the Lord Jesus as your wisdom? How much do your really know the Lord Jesus? This is a basic question.

Let us be quite clear: It does not say here that the Lord Jesus gives us wisdom, nor does it say that God gives the wisdom of the Lord Jesus to us as though we are rather foolish but that now with the wisdom God gives us we begin to know how to speak and to act. No, the Bible never puts it that way. What it says is that God has made Christ our wisdom. "Was made" are two very important words here. None can be better than these two words.

Let us illustrate this with Moses and Aaron. Moses would not go to the children of Israel and speak to them, fearful lest his eloquence be inadequate. He said he was slow of speech, therefore he dared not go. How did God answer him? "Is there not Aaron thy brother the Levite? . . . He shall be thy spokesman unto the people; . . . he shall be to thee a mouth" (Ex. 4.14,16). Now was it because Aaron had become a mouth to Moses that therefore the eloquence of Moses was suddenly increased? Not at all. Aaron became a mouth to Moses, but Moses remained the same (How well Moses spoke later on, of course, is another matter). Whenever Moses' eloquence proved inadequate, he could call on Aaron to speak for him. And this was how he became Moses' mouth. The eloquence was still in Aaron's mouth, not in Moses' mouth. Moses needed Aaron to be his mouth because his own was inadequate. Yet Moses' mouth did not become activated because he had accepted Aaron to be his mouth.

Thus can we understand how God makes Christ our wisdom. It does not mean that Christ has made us wise; it simply means that recognizing our own foolishness we cease to move ourselves but allow the Lord to be our wisdom. Formerly, whenever there was outside demand, our own life would rise up to react; today when there is such outside demand we know how inadequate we are, and so we let the life of the Lord react instead. Not that we ourselves have then become adequate, but that the Lord comes in to live for us. Not that Moses' mouth has improved in eloquence, but that Aaron had replaced him as his mouth to speak for him.

For Christ to be our wisdom can be likened to Aaron's speaking on behalf of Moses. Let us suppose you go out to talk to people and you find yourself speechless; what can you do? You ask the one who goes with you to speak on your behalf. You cannot speak, so you ask him to speak for you. He supplies the demand on your behalf. And while he is speaking eloquently your mouth remains as slow of speech as before, without the slightest improvement. Never mistakenly conceive, therefore, that because Christ has become our wisdom we thereby grow wise ourselves. Always remember that though we have Christ as our wisdom, our own selves remain inadequate.*

"It is no longer I that live, but Christ liveth in me" (Gal. 2.20). This is a fact. It shows us how to be a Christian. That is, I do nothing but let Christ himself do everything. In other words, with Aaron as mouth, you, Moses, need not open yours. Let us suppose you know someone who is not able to speak, and yet speak he must. So, you suggest to him: let me speak for you. Nevertheless, while you are speaking, he shows his unhappiness by injecting a word or two; with the result

---

*Let us be aware, however, that there are two sides to this matter. True, when Christ dwells in us and lives for us, the one who lives is Christ. It is He who lives out through me. I am only responsible for obeying Him and not hindering Him. There is also another side: that after passing through a long period of obedience and cooperation, and being penetrated and moulded by the life of Christ for many years, the nature of this glorious life is gradually incorporated into my soul. Unconsciously a second personality is being produced in me. During that time, I undergo a substantial change. And this is the work of the Holy Spirit in making precious stones. It also is from glory—the glory of the Lord—to glory. All areas of my soul are gradually being glorified (see 2 Cor. 3.18).—*Author*

that you have to say more to cover what he says. Does not this make you feel most embarrassed? If a Moses is slow in speech, he should accept an Aaron's mouth as his. Thank God, this is precisely the salvation of the Lord. Long ago God did not change Moses' mouth; He simply gave him a new mouth. And God today does not change anyone's mouth; He merely gives a new mouth. He does not make the foolish wise; He makes Christ the wisdom of the foolish. And this is real salvation.

An example of what has been said might be as follows: A certain matter arises which requires great wisdom to manage it well. You exhaust what little brain power you possess and still find it unresolved. So you pray: "O Lord, I truly am foolish. If this is left to me, I am sure I will fail. I can only look to You to do it for me." After you have in this way wholly trusted the Lord, you will be amazed at His wisdom in moving you to do and to speak. In looking back you will one day exclaim: "Ah, what I did on that day is truly what I could not do myself. What I said that day is really what I personally would never be able to say." This indicates that you yourself have not changed, only that the Lord has become your wisdom. This reveals how Christ is made wisdom to us. Previously I was required to meet a situation which in my own wisdom I could not handle, but now I let Christ come forth to be my wisdom.

We must ever keep in mind that it is not Christ's wisdom made our wisdom, nor is it Christ giving us wisdom to make us wise, rather is it Christ himself being made wisdom to us. Consequently, all the wisdom belongs to the Lord, none to us. He himself becomes our wisdom. If in truth we understand what is meant by Christ being made wisdom to us, we shall be able to live a life well-pleasing to God.

2 Christ Is Made Our Righteousness

We mentioned earlier that the fact of Christ being made our wisdom includes three things—righteousness, sanctification, and redemption. Let us begin with righteousness.*

One

Righteousness is what we need before God: for righteousness is closely related to God. If we never come before Him, we do not consider the matter of righteousness or unrighteousness. But the moment we do think of God, we immediately realize this problem.

---

* See Chapter Two of Part One above for a more thorough discussion by the author of Christ as our righteousness. Although what is mentioned in this present Chapter may seem to be repetitious, it was thought helpful to include it nevertheless so as to provide the reader with the full picture the author had in mind when in his presentation of Christ having been made our *wisdom* he briefly touches upon righteousness as being the first of three complementary aspects of that wisdom.—*Translator*

For example, when we go to visit people we always think of our dress. Now in the same way, when anyone thinks of approaching God, he must have righteousness, because without it he cannot meet God. For this reason, righteousness is a fundamental issue in Christian living. The issue is: On what ground does anyone draw near to God each time? If a Christian has not clearly solved this problem of righteousness he has a shaky foundation.

No Christian can come to God with bold assurance if he is still doubtful about righteousness. Many Christians wish to grow and would gladly walk in the way of God, yet they simply go round and round without making any progress. Why? One of the reasons is that they are not perfectly clear on this question of righteousness. Though this is elementary, it is nonetheless essential. We must be clear on this point, otherwise we cannot walk peacefully but will always have trouble.

Two

Often we do not know on what ground we draw nigh to God. Many times we think our good works are the righteousness by which we come to Him. Some brothers and sisters reflect that they have righteousness today because from morning till night they have done well; or else if their works are not perfect their righteousness becomes defective. To such minds, their righteousness is their works.

One day, though, God opens our eyes to see that our righteousness before Him is not our works but is something else. He uses His light as a knife to sever works from righteousness. Previously we deemed our works to be our righteousness before God, now we come to Him with Christ as our righteousness. Hereafter our righteousness is no longer our works, hereafter in His presence our righteousness is Christ. My works *may be* improved, but my righteousness cannot be bettered. My works are never perfect, yet my righteousness is always perfect. My righteousness is Christ by whom I draw near to God. My works are subject to criticism; but thank God, my righteousness is beyond criticism for it is none other than Christ.

Three

To know Christ as our righteousness is a great salvation. God has solved for us the problem of righteousness, and thus our standing before Him is settled. Yes, we should have good works, we should do all things well, we should serve the Lord diligently, and we should take up the cross; nevertheless, we should understand that though our works may advance greatly, our righteousness before God cannot be improved upon. What we depend on to come to Him today is that which we shall depend on even after ten or twenty years. For our righteousness before God is not our works, but Christ. Unless one has received revelation —seeing Christ as his righteousness—he cannot draw nigh to God with boldness. If he sees that his righteousness is a person who is Christ, he can come without fear. Hence we must never forget that when we approach God, our righteousness is not our works, it is not a thing; it is a person, even Christ.

3 Christ Is Made Our Sanctification

We now come to a further point in our discussion together. To say that my righteousness before God is not my works does not suggest that I need not be careful of my conduct or works while living on earth. My problem of righteousness before God is indeed solved, but how about my conduct and my living? Here must you and I see that God has not only made Christ my righteousness but has also made Him my sanctification. This sanctification is not a thing, nor a condition, but again, it is a person—even Christ.

One

Some Christians entertain a kind of mental ideal about sanctification. They envisage sanctification to be Christ helping us, then transforming us into holiness. Formerly we were unholy, now through the help which Christ gives us we become holy. 1 Corinthians 1.30, however, tells us that God has made Christ our sanctification. We do not rely on our own strength to be holy, nor do we count on the help of Christ to be holy, we trust Christ himself to be our holiness. Our sanctification is the *person* of Christ, not the *help* of Christ.

Some Christians think that Christ gives us strength to be holy. Hence they pray to the Lord for strength. They reckon that by receiving strength they will be holy. However, the word of God never says we can be holy, nor does it say Christ gives us strength to be holy. It plainly tells us that God has made Christ our sanctification. Our sanctification is a Gift, our sanctification is a Person; our sanctification is not the result of some God-given strength. If we do not see with our spiritual eyes, we will not know what immense difference exists here. This is something our brain can never comprehend. Had there been no revelation, and even if our brain could somehow grasp it, it would still be of little use. We must ask God to show us that Christ has not come to help us to be holy, nor does He give us strength to be holy, but He himself becomes our holiness.

Two

With respect to this subject of sanctification, many believers understand it in two regards: one is called the power of sanctification and the other is called the fruit of sanctification. What they mean is that one must possess the power of sanctification in order to produce the fruit thereof. According to this concept, where will Christ be—is He on the power side or is He on the fruit side? The way 1 Corinthians 1.30 presents it is totally contrary to man's concept. It teaches us that Christ does not come to be the power of our sanctification, instead He himself *is* our sanctification. He does not come to be the power of our sanctification so as to cause us to produce sanctification. No, it is simply that because we have Christ we therefore have sanctification. If we view holiness as a thing, then the word of God tells us that Christ is that thing. Our thing is a living Person, our holiness is a living Person. The thing we have is Christ, for our sanctification is Christ.

Let us use humility as an illustration. Suppose I am very proud. Not that I am not conscious of my pride, but that I just cannot be humble. So I ask God: "O God, have mercy on me. Send the Lord Jesus to me to help me that I may be humble." Do see here that I am taking Christ as help towards humility because, as I conceive it, with the help of Christ I can be humble: yet this is my idea, not God's salvation. God has not given Christ to me to help me to be humble; what He gives to me is Christ as my humility. God has not given us Christ as the power of humility to cause us to produce humility in our lives; rather has He given us Christ to be our humility.

Just reflect for a moment: Does the Lord have the power? We all know He has the power. Has He given this power to us? Yes, He has given us this power. Why, then, are we so weak and feeble? Let it be known that even were the Lord to give us all His power, we would not know how to use it. His power is real, but we do not know how to utilize it. We fancy we can be humble through the power of the Lord, nonetheless we find we still are not humble. The work we can accomplish is to have an outward behavior called humility, though within us there is no such thing as humility. The word of God shows us that our humility is Christ, not the power of Christ.

What does it mean to say that our humility is the Lord himself? It means I have no humility, and I cannot be humble; even if the Lord gives me power, I still do not know how to be humble. I can only say to Him: "Lord, you are my humility, I allow you to be my humility." For Christ to be my humility simply means to let Him manifest His own humility in my stead.

When we ask God to give us power to be humble, we may perhaps be able to be humble for a short while, yet this humility is but a good work, a good attitude, a good intention, a good deportment. It is not Christ. But when we ask the Lord to be our humility, we look up and say to Him: "Lord, there is no humility in me. Even if you give me power I still cannot be humble. Therefore, O Lord, You be my humility, you be humble for me." After you have looked to the Lord in this way and you begin to be humble, you immediately discover how natural is this humility. Your humility is not a work but a living person, even Christ himself.

The same is true with patience: I have no patience, I am not able to be patient, my patience is Christ himself. It is also true of meekness: I have no meekness, I do not know how to be meek, my meekness is Christ himself. Have you now seen that God has made Christ my patience and my meekness? All our virtues are Christ. Christian virtue is quite different from commonly know virtue. The latter is one thing after another, whereas the former is not in fragments but is a living person, Christ himself. Our virtue is not in plural but in singular number; our virtue is not in many fragmentary things; it is a Person. Simply stated, if we do not know Christ, we will have nothing at all.

Three

Christ in us as our life reacts on our behalf against all outside demands. Life itself is one, but it produces all kinds of reaction to meet all sorts of outside requirements. When there is pride, Christ will be my humility if He is released at that hour. When there is impatience, Christ will be my patience in His direct manifestation. When there is jealousy, Christ will be my love in His immediate expression. From this one Life comes forth many virtues. Due to a variety of circumstantial demands the manifestations of this Life are also various. Daily do we meet all kinds of situations; in all of them Christ manifests himself as many virtues. Hence the virtues of a Christian are not his works but are the reflections or manifestations of Christ. This we call Christ our sanctification.

For this reason, our entire living as Christians depends on how much we know Christ. It is not a matter of whether I am humble or not, patient or not, meek or not; it is totally a matter of Christ. The more I know Him the more will the manifestations of the virtues of a Christian be Christ. And thus will we see that our virtues are simply Christ being released through us. The patience of brother Chen is Christ. The love of brother Chow is also Christ, so too are the meekness of sister Wu and the humility of sister Liu. All these various virtues are Christ. People are different, the manifestation of virtues varies, but the source of all is Christ.

Hallelujah, all our virtues are Christ; whatever issues forth from us is Christ. The love that flows from brother Chow is Christ, the meekness which comes out of sister Wu is Christ, and the humility which is manifested in sister Liu is also Christ. The demands of environment are not the same, yet the inward supplies are identical. The outward expressions are many, but the substance is one. None of the virtues of a Christian is his own work but is the outflow of Christ within. These virtues are the reflections of Christ through us. And once you and I perceive this we will look up to the Lord and say, "Formerly I relied on myself to be a Christian, and I was wrong. Lord, I thank You, for now I know You are my sanctification. I will let You live through me."

4 | Christ Is Made Our Redemption

God has not only made Christ our righteousness and our sanctification. He has also made Christ our redemption. The meaning of redemption is to redeem back or to redeem out. In this discussion of redemption, three elements are imperative: namely, the redeemed, the Redeemer, and the redeeming cost. All who are redeemed were once sold to sin (Rom. 7.14) and were therefore slaves to sin. But now the Lord Jesus has paid the price of His blood (Matt. 20.28; Mark 10.45; 1 Tim. 2.6) to redeem us out of the curse of the law (Gal. 3.13). Herein do we know that the Lord Jesus is our Redeemer.

One

We will go a step further, however, to see that the Lord Jesus is our redemption as He also is our Redeemer. If the Lord Jesus is only our Redeemer, and though the relationship thus created between the Redeemer and the redeemed is most intimate, the two sides are still separated. Yet the Lord is not only our Redeemer, He is also our redemption. This means that in being redeemed we are not only related to a thing, we are even more so related to a Person. Since we are the redeemed, the Lord joins himself with us into one. Our redemption is a Person: having Him, we have redemption: not having Him, there is no redemption. To put it another way, If we wish to have redemption, we must have Him; for only in having Him do we have redemption, since He is redemption. Our redemption is therefore not a thing, Our redemption is a Person, One who unites with us.

With Christ as our redemption, we who are cleansed by the precious blood of the Lord may approach God with boldness. When God judges sinners He can justly pass over all who have the blood of the Lamb (Ex. 12.12,13; Rom. 3.25,26). All the redeemed are redeemed completely. When God looks down upon us, all He sees is Christ. It may be said that He sees no man but Christ only. Christ is the Lamb slain, His precious blood has settled man's crime before God. None who approaches God through Christ will be condemned, since Christ has already satisfied the righteous demand of God on man's behalf in His receiving the penalty of man's sin. All who have Christ have redemption. Seeing Christ, God sees redemption.

Two

Christ is made our redemption *in us* as well as *before God*. His being made our redemption in us is especially related to our body. In being our redemption in us He becomes the life of our body as He delivers us from the law of sin which is in our members (Rom. 7.23, 8.2). So says Romans 8.11: "If the Spirit of him that raised up Jesus from the dead dwelleth in you, he that raised up Christ Jesus from the dead shall give life also to your mortal bodies through his Spirit that dwelleth in you." It does not say He shall resurrect us after we die; it says instead that He will give life to this our body of death today.

Look also at 2 Corinthians 4.10,11 which reads as follows: "Always bearing about in the body the dying of Jesus, that the life also of Jesus may be manifested in our body. For we who live are always delivered unto death for Jesus' sake, that the life also of Jesus may be manifested in our mortal flesh." What arrests our attention here is that though verse 11 in relation to verse 10 seems to be redundant, in actuality it is not repetitious. For verse 10 speaks of the life of Jesus being manifested *in our body,* while verse 11 speaks of the life of Jesus being manifested *in our mortal flesh.* Many believers may have the life of Jesus manifested in them, but they do not go deeper to experience the life of Jesus manifested in their mortal flesh. The difference between these two is immense.

Many believers while in sickness may be truly submissive and patient. They are neither anxious nor murmuring. They sense the presence of the Lord, and they express in their face, voice and manners the virtues of the Lord Jesus. They really manifest the life of Jesus in their body by the Holy Spirit. Nevertheless, they do not know that the Lord Jesus is able to heal their sickness, that His life is also for their bodies of humiliation. They have received the grace to endure pains, but they have not obtained the healing of the Lord. They experience verse 10, yet they do not experience verse 11.

We need to know how Christ is made our redemption in relation to our body. To say that this our body of death is quickened into life does not imply that hereafter the nature of this body is changed into immortality. As a matter of fact, the nature of this body remains unchanged, though a new life in us is now supplying strength to this body. Formerly we relied on our natural life as the source of our body strength, but presently we depend on the life of Christ for its supply. We obtain the resurrection life of Christ to maintain our body, thus strengthened to do God's will.

Three

Christ our redemption is not a small matter. Being our redemption, Christ not only becomes today the life of our body but also gives us a great hope, even "the redemption of our body" (Rom. 8.21-23; 1 Cor. 15.50-54; Phil. 3.21). One day, God will reveal how He has redeemed the creation and how we are His. At that day our body will be fully redeemed. It will put off corruptibility and put on incorruptibility. It will be delivered from the bondage of corruption and enter into the liberty of glory. Then, the dead will be raised, and we shall all be changed. This body of our humiliation will be transformed and be conformed to the body of Christ's glory. At that time we shall fully realize how Christ is our redemption! Who has the assurance of having a part in the first resurrection? Who has the certainty that one day his body will be changed? We do believe, and therefore we have the confidence. It is all because Christ is our redemption.

We are told in 1 Corinthians 15.42-44 that after a Christian is dead, he is not to be buried, but is to be "sown". We know how totally contrary burying is from sowing. If, for instance, you bury a piece of copper beneath the earth, it is buried because it will never grow up. But, if you sow a seed into the ground, it will come out after certain days. After a Christian is dead, he is not buried in the earth as a piece of copper, but like a grain of wheat he is sown into the ground and will one day come up again. He will rise again because the life of Christ is in him, which life cannot be held by death. A born-again Christian has Christ in him, and Christ is his redemption. His resurrected body is incorruptible, glorious, strong, and spiritual.

Furthermore, due to the fact that Christ is made redemption to us, some Christians may possibly not see death. This is rapture. On one occasion a little girl asked a preacher, "Is it difficult for a Christian to be raptured?" To this child's mind, rapture must require much effort. We know, however, that rapture is quite different from our human concept. A believer is raptured because he has Christ in him. Christ being his redemption will carry him up.

Four

Christ as our life is the foundation of a Christian.

The first step in our salvation is regeneration, and the last step is the redemption of the body. From beginning to end, everything is based on Christ as our life. The relationship between Him and us is that of life. In other words, it is an indissoluble relationship. Christ does not come to be some outward things to us. He comes to enter into us to be our life. The relationship of life is an eternal bond. In case we do not have Christ as our life, we have no relationship with Him at all. Yet possessing Him as our life, our union with Him is indissoluble.

We observe how after Adam sinned, God instantly guarded the way to the tree of life with cherubim and flame of sword which turned every way. Why? Because should Adam also eat the fruit of the tree of life, he would have a relationship with God that could not be dissolved. Thank God, our union with Christ today is that which Adam in the beginning never had. It is an eternal, indestructible relationship, such that even God himself has no way to dissolve it. This life abides in us and will bring us into glory, into eternity. This is the exceeding greatness of His power! This is the hope of glory!

In conclusion, then, let us ask God to open our eyes that we may see how He has already put us in Christ and has also made Christ our wisdom, even righteousness and sanctification and redemption. May God show us that of all His gifts to us, there is nothing greater than His own Son. May He reveal to us how

Christ is the gift and the gifts. Christ is the gift in the singular as well as the many gifts in the plural. We must learn to know Him as our wisdom—both our righteousness, our sanctification, and our redemption. May the Lord deliver us from foolishness and darkness and enable us to know that in spiritual things we have nothing but Christ.

PART THREE

THE POWER OF HIS RESURRECTION

1 Dead to the Law

Wherefore, my brethren, ye also were made dead to the law through the body of Christ; that ye should be joined to another, even to him who was raised from the dead, that we might bring forth fruit unto Gcd. (Rom. 7.4)

For that which I do I know not: for not what I would, that do I practise; but what I hate, that I do. But if what I would not, that I do, I consent unto the law that it is good. So now it is no more I that do it, but sin which dwelleth in me. For I know that in me, that is, in my flesh, dwelleth no good thing: for to will is present with me, but to do that which is good is not. For the good which I would I do not: but the evil which I would not, that I practise. (Rom. 7.15-19)

Romans 7 is a chapter which we are most familiar with, not only in the reading of it but also in the experiencing of it. We frequently read Romans 7, and how often we live Romans 7. What God wants us to know is how we can be delivered from the demand of the law, or in other words, how we can be delivered from ourselves.

One

Before we discuss this subject of deliverance and the way of deliverance, we must first mention a condition or qualification of those to be delivered. Even though God's deliverance is prepared for all, not all are delivered. Everyone *may* be delivered from the law, but not everyone *is* delivered. The problem is not on God's side, it is instead on man's side, for not all men desire such deliverance nor are all willing to pay the cost. The apostle in his experience of Romans 7 finally becomes emancipated only because he has fulfilled the condition of knowing what to hate as well as what to desire.

The most urgent problem here, then, is this: that before you can be delivered, is there to be found in you a strong aversion to that temper which you just cannot overcome, to that sin which defeats you all the time, or to that particular point where you always fall? You may presume to believe that sinning is something quite common to all Christians and is therefore unavoidable. Or you may assume the proper attitude of abhorring such condition before God and of asking to be delivered from sinful acts, unclean thoughts, an uncontrollable temper, and wicked passions. The apostle mentions in this chapter 7 not only how he gets released *but also how he feels in his heart before he is released.* Before he is delivered, how strongly he hates what he does: "For not what I would, that do I practise; but what I hate, that I do" (v.15). Hence the first and foremost question today is: Do you love what you are doing now, or do you hate what you are doing now? We know the apostle becomes liberated because he deeply hates and desperately asks. He is so unwilling to live a life in sin that he is determined to get out of it. He hates his situation so much that he would rather die than to have it extended any longer. Due to his determination, he receives deliverance.

Do you have such a hungry heart today? Do you really find it impossible to continue on being a Christian in this manner? Can you live on if you are still held by sin and not delivered? Have you seen the horror of your condition? What the Lord has burdened me with in this manner is directed towards those who really desire deliverance, those who truly consider their Christian life to be below par. It is not for those who are self-complacent—who are content to live in defeat and sin. It is for those who seek but have yet to find the way, not for those who regard bursts of temper, lustful impulses, and unclean thoughts as insignificant and deceive themselves into thinking that as long as they confess their sins God will surely forgive and thus everything will be all right. The victory of Romans 7 is for those who have experienced the defeats of Romans 7. Unless there is an abhorrence towards the current condition plus an aversion towards ever continuing in such a situation, there can be no victory.

All who live a life of defeat and sin without repudiating it will not experience the deliverance of God.

Let it be remembered that each time there is spiritual progress in your life before God it invariably is preceded by a dissatisfaction with your current condition. All progress starts from dissatisfaction. You must be pressed to a point where you feel you have come to the end and that you just cannot continue on any longer. Such kind of life is so abnormal that you find it impossible to live on under the triple bondage of self, the world, and sin. "Not what I would, that do I practise; but what I hate, that I do"—this type of paradoxical life should not exist. A way out must be found. And to those people who are in such a crisis God will reveal what deliverance is. There is therefore the great need of going before God and asking Him for grace that He would not allow you to live comfortably in this life of sin and defeat. The starting point for each victory is at that moment when you begin to hate your defeat. Whoever is to be delivered needs to be pressed beyond the measure of tolerance. Only such a person as this is open to deliverance.

Two

What I am now going to share is but the way to deliverance; only God can give actual deliverance. In other words, what I here communicate is only light, but what God gives to you directly is alone revelation. Light cannot deliver you, only revelation can.

Romans 7 is a tremendous chapter. It not being

appropriate, in so short a space, to comment on the whole chapter, I will select but one particular verse for our primary consideration. And that is verse 4. It first mentions this: "Wherefore, my brethren, ye also were made dead to the law . . ." Do we recognize that we need to be delivered from the law? If I were to say we need to be saved from sins we all would understand this because we all know the dreadfulness of sins. If I were to say we must be freed from the world, this we too would comprehend because we see that the world is so wicked as to have crucified our Lord. If I were to say we should be delivered from self, this we also would appreciate because we recognize that the flesh is truly most abhorrent. But when the writer says here that it is needful for us to be delivered from the law, we may not feel very much concerning its need in our lives. If the apostle had said, Be delivered from self, we would have responded with an amen; or, Be delivered from the world, we again would have responded with an amen; or, Be delivered from sins and uncleanness, we once more would have responded the same way. But when he says, Be delivered from the law by being dead to it, we do not know what to answer. We trust that whatever the apostle says must be right; nevertheless, we are puzzled over why he says it. We know the reasons why we must be delivered from sins, self, and the world; yet we do not understand why we should be delivered from the law. Why does the apostle call for us to be dead to the law so as to be freed from it? Is there any relationship between a being delivered from the law and being delivered from the world, from sins, and from self? The relationship is indeed great!

Let us see that one thing is needful for any Christian who is seeking after deliverance: he must first of all know that God has absolutely no hope in him and therefore he ought equally to regard himself as being hopeless. He must be clear as to what assessment God has of him as well as what assessment he has of himself. We are all Christians, for we all belong to Christ. Some of us may be Christians who have been such for many years. We have had our times of failure and have also experienced many stumblings and driftings. But what do we do after each defeat? Almost to a man, after each failure there is a renewed determination. We say to ourselves, "Next time I will be better, I will not fall again!" Yet each defeat also brings in fresh grief. We blame ourselves saying, "Why did I do it? Why do I always fall? I am a believer, I should not be that bad!" We are very much grieved. Hence nearly everyone after a defeat will arrive at these two consequences: one, he wills to do better in the future; and two, he grieves at the past and sighs. These are the things we all usually do. Oftentimes immediately after a failure we cry with anguish, "Why am I so mean? I will never do it next time. O Lord, deliver me!"

Such an experience is similar to that of Romans 7. The trouble is, though, that before the first grief ends, the chance for new grief already arrives. Before the first determination is carried out, the next determination has to be made. Time after time this happens without any improvement. This, then, is our situation.

Yet why is this so? It is because we have not been delivered from the law. We have not seen what the law is, nor have we understood what deliverance from the law means.

In order to know how to be delivered from the law, we must first understand the relationship between the law and us. The law is God's demands on our flesh. By the law God tells us what is right and what is wrong, what we should do and what we should not do, what is forbidden and what is commanded. Hence the law is God's demands on us. Or to phrase it another way, the law is God's demands on all who are in Adam. It is His commandments to all who are in Adam as to what they ought not to do. (The purpose of God's giving the law is to prove the corruption of the flesh which is beyond cure.) Let us remember that not only can God put us under the law, we too who are in Adam may also place ourselves under the law with a view to pleasing God. This means we may set up rules and regulations for ourselves to keep, by which we are saying: I ought not do this and I ought to do that. Besides the commandments given us by God, we also lay down commandments for ourselves to keep, and they are as strict as God's. Consequently, we have demands on ourselves as well as God has demands on us. All this indicates that we still have hope in this man that is in Adam. We continue to expect him to strive to be better and more victorious. This, in sum, is our current situation: God puts us under the law, and we put ourselves under the law.

What is meant by being delivered from the law? It

is to be totally disillusioned about yourself. Not only to be fully disappointed, but also to expect nothing anymore. Henceforth you no longer entertain any hope in yourself. This is a being delivered from the law. God, as it were, allows you to sin day after day in order to make you realize how corrupted and unclean, how unamendable and unconquering you really are, how unable you are to keep the law because you are beyond any help. He wants you to know why He has crucified you in Christ and with Christ. It is because you are corrupted beyond cure. When you finally see yourself helpless, as well as understand that God considers you hopeless, you will then stand on the ground which God has given you. God says you are corrupted to the core and there is absolutely no hope for you; you too say you are so corrupted and helpless that you can only sin, therefore you entertain no hope in yourself. Now this is a being delivered from the law. And what a great deliverance it truly is. *The one and only deliverance is a seeing yourself as being utterly hopeless.*

Once I met a dear brother in the Lord, a Mr. Keil. He was good with respect to the gospel, and he was used by God to win many souls. At that time he was already 60. One day as we were strolling along, we talked about this matter. He said these lessons should always be taught. I asked him what he meant. He answered thus: "Speaking of my past history, when I was a young believer, I was really most zealous and truly expected to serve the Lord well. I wished to make progress all the time for I wished Keil to do well. But things turned out differently. My situation went from bad to worse: I saw myself being increasingly unable. I was so disappointed, and was truly surprised at my inability. One day a brother spoke to me, saying, 'Mr. Keil, God does not expect what you expect of yourself. You yourself have so much hope, yet God has no hope in you.' I was amazed at such words, and I therefore asked him what God said about me. This brother's answer was this: 'God knows how you are without strength, that you cannot do anything, and that you are completely helpless. And this is why He crucified you. So that you are fit for nothing but to be crucified.' Since that day, as though scales had fallen from my eyes, I can now really see that God has absolutely no demand on me. I today know I can do nothing, and therefore God has had me crucified. Why, then, should I strive anymore?"

Even though we know quite well in theory and in teaching that the old Adamic life is unamendable and beyond cure, yet strange to say, when it comes to experience, we still entertain hope in this Adamic life and try to amend and to improve it. Many of us are saying, I am surprised I could commit such a sin! May we be reminded that we should not be surprised at all. What sin will we *not* commit? We can commit *any* sin because the root of sin is in us. God crucified us because He saw we were, and still are, helpless and hopeless. So that when the Lord died, we too died. That God has crucified us reveals His estimate of us. Except for death or for being cast aside, we are not fit for anything.

How different is our own appraisal from God's. We always think we are able and that we can. We consider ourselves capable of victory, sanctification, and progress. But God expects nothing of these from us. He declares that from head to foot our whole being is full of sins and we are altogether useless. Apart from death there is no salvation. Today we should see this basic fact of how God looks at us and what He thinks we deserve. Whoever sees this first is blessed.

How many Christians begin to see that God has absolutely no hope in them *only after* they have suffered many falls, encountered many defeats, and in their walk have traversed many irretrievable miles! The earlier we see this fact the better. For actual deliverances begin here. Indeed, the release of the true life also starts from here: to see ourselves before God as fit for nothing but death. The earlier we see this the quicker the progress. The entire problem revolves around our conclusion with regard to the old Adamic life. No doubt we all know how unamendable and irredeemable is this old Adamic life; nevertheless, I may ask how few really see they ought to die—how few actually acknowledge that apart from death there is no alternative. Knowing the teaching is one thing, understanding and seeing is another. Teaching is comprehended by the mind, but seeing must be revealed in the spirit. All which is without revelation and seeing is not counted because there will be no effect.

To be delivered from the law is to be delivered from God's demand, which means that, having known the work of Christ as well as the life of Adam, we give up the idea of trying to please God. As long as there is in our heart the thought of seeking progress and pleasing God by our own effort, we are not delivered from the law nor are we exempt from sorrow and despair. Knowing that God does not expect anything from us is the only way not to despair.

We need to be delivered from the law; but how? It is only through death. Why is death capable of freeing us from the law. Because as long as we *live*, the law has its demand on us. A living person must not violate the law inasmuch as he will be prosecuted if he does. This is exactly what the apostle means by this statement: "For the woman that hath a husband is bound by law to the husband while he liveth" (Rom. 7.2). If the husband still lives, the law has its claim on the woman; but if he dies, the influence of the law ceases and it demands no more. Therefore, apart from death there is no other way to be liberated from the law. For if we live, the law will keep on demanding of us.

Now let us turn from how the law of God makes its claim on us to how we set up law to make demand on ourselves. When do you charge yourself? At the moment when you rise up quite late today you make up your mind that you will get up early tomorrow. Or when you realize how unclean is your life as you struggle from dawn to dusk in the whirlpool of sin and of the world, do you not will to overcome hereafter? You always think you may and you can. Thus, you see *yourself* as very much alive. The work of *Christ* cannot be manifested in you.

But if you really know God that He has given you

up (in fact, the only thing He can do with you is to crucify you), and if you realize that you are fit for nothing but death, then you will not make any resolution. This is what had happened to me. How I frequently willed never to do it again. But then I asked myself: Am I worthy of death? If so, why will at all? Hence let us see that the way of victory is not in resolution but by standing on the ground which God has given us. Do not hope for better next time, but stand on what ground God may give us. We should no longer make any resolution, neither expect progress nor strive for victory—because we know all these come from the old Adamic life. We instead will put it to death: we will ignore it altogether. As we truly stand on the ground of death we triumph and are set free from every bondage. Consequently, death is our only way out. Neither the world nor sin nor self nor anything else can touch a person who is dead. If we reckon ourselves as dead, we will be beyond the reach of any of these things.

Three

Let us go a step further and see how we die. "Wherefore, my brethren, ye also were made dead to the law through the body of Christ . . ." Our death is through the body of Christ. As Christ himself died, so we died also. The time when Christ died is when we died. Since Christ has died, we too have died. This is not committing spiritual suicide, nor do we reckon ourselves as dead arbitrarily, attempting to hypnotize ourselves to death. No, it is because we have seen the accomplished fact of Christ on the cross. We therefore know that God has already included us in the death of Christ. When we see this, we cannot help but acknowledge ourselves as being dead.

There are two spiritual experiences in the world which are most amazing. One is seeing God's plan; that is to say, seeing what God has planned for you and what He designs you to be—to wit, God has sentenced you to death. The other amazing experience is seeing what God has done for you in Christ. These two spiritual facts are exceedingly great, that you can see what God has determined for you and also see how you are united in one with Christ, thus enjoying in Him all that He has accomplished. For instance, when Jesus Christ died on the cross you were there too, because God had included you in His death. And when His body was broken you too were broken. His crucifixion is your crucifixion, since you and Christ are one. For this reason we are careful about baptism.

Many people suggest that baptism is only an outward ritual, therefore unimportant. Not so. Baptism is a full testimony to what has happened within. We believe that when Christ died, we too have died. The first thing after death will be burial. So by water baptism we are buried. If we do not believe we are dead we will not consent to be buried. Our assent to our being buried is because we believe we are dead. Baptism, then, is a burial performed on the basis of believing both the death of Christ and the death of ourselves. Burial proves that we are dead. To illustrate: When the veil was rent, the cherubim embroidered on the veil were also rent. Just as the veil was rent from top to bottom by God, so the cherubim were rent by God from top to bottom. We know the veil represents the body of Christ (see Heb. 10.20). The cherubim are God's created beings. When Christ died, the whole creation of God died too. This is the meaning of our being made dead to the law through the body of Christ.

The way of deliverance lies not in a forced reckoning of ourselves as dead. Such teaching of forced reckoning is erroneous. What, then, is the correct way? It is reckoning ourselves as dead *in Christ.* Not that we die ourselves, but that we were made dead through the body of Christ. Since Christ has died, and we are united with Him, therefore we too have died. *The secret of victory is a never looking at ourselves outside of Christ.* This is what Christ means by the words "Abide in Me" found in John 15. It is never to look at ourselves outside of Christ. There is nothing good to be looked at outwardly, and these ugly sights cannot be improved either. If we want to look at ourselves we can only look at ourselves in the Lord. As soon as we look at the self outside of Christ we immediately fall. How often we forget the accomplished fact of Christ. We become angry with ourselves, saying, "How can I do this?" We always fail, we constantly fall. We bemoan ourselves and lose heart. Yet let us recognize the fact that all these things are done by the self that is outside of Christ. In Christ we are dead to the law. In case anyone among us has not known this deliverance, why not let that person look at himself in Christ today? In Christ God has had us crucified. He regards us as irreparable, hence there is no salvation except death. He has sentenced us to death and has also crucified us in Christ. We are now delivered from the claim of the law. We are free.

We must absolutely stand on these two facts. First, God sees that apart from death there is no other way to deliver us from the law. Second, God has already crucified us in Christ. The first speaks of God's plan, and the second, of God's work. The first is a decision, the second is an accomplishment. We have been broken into tiny fragments beyond the possibility of being made whole. Aside from death there is no salvation. Hence the foundation of redemption is in the cross. How we must accept this fact in our daily life so as to be delivered from the law. If we stand firm on this ground we will prosper. Of course you and I must confess and ask God for forgiveness when we fail. Nevertheless, we do not need to cast another look at the past since all our defeats and falls derive from the old Adamic life. Should we ask the Lord to give us strength so that we will not do it again, to men this looks excellent but to God this is unnecessary because we have died in Christ. Our history has ended, and therefore none of our decisions and desires count. How people always deem the making of a resolution to be the best thing in life, not knowing that it is like a reed which cannot withstand the enemy nor has any use before God.

Four

We have seen how God has crucified us with Christ. But this alone is not sufficient. So we have the following word: "... that ye should be joined to another, even to him who was raised from the dead, that we might bring forth fruit unto God"—and thus we have not only the negative deliverance but also the positive joining, otherwise all will still be in vain. God has not only crucified us, He has also joined us—who have been delivered from the law—to Christ, who was raised from the dead. The one is a coming out, whereas the other is an entering in. The one is the *severance* of a relationship, while the other is the *establishing* of a relationship. It is a being delivered from the law on the one hand and a being joined to Christ on the other. And this latter is what we mean by resurrection. Resurrection is a being joined with Christ, yet not the joining of *one* but rather the joining of *many* to Christ. Resurrection is the bringing of many sons into glory. This is what is alluded to in John 12: "Except a grain of wheat fall into the earth and die, it abideth by itself alone; but if it die, it beareth much fruit" (v.24). Originally there is only one life; now this life enters into many grains. Originally there is but one grain of wheat; now it has multiplied to become many grains. Likewise, Christ through death distributes His life to all believers. Thus, there are two facts in Christ: one is that God has included us in the death of Christ, and therefore when Christ died, we too died; the other is that we are raised together with Christ from the dead, thus receiving His imparted life. These are what all regenerated persons possess and possess together.

We who are resurrected in Christ will bring forth fruit to the glory of God. Since God has given the life of Christ to us, we hereafter are able to live out Christ's life. Whatever be the grain of wheat that is sown, there shall be the thirty, the sixty or the hundred grains which grow out of it. If a person plants barley he will not get wheat or squash. What is sown is that which grows. There can be no change. If what is sown is wheat, all which grows out will be wheat. How can we live like Christ and bear fruit to glorify God as Christ did? In only one way: by letting Christ live in us and letting Him live out of us. Consequently, Christ not only died for us on the cross but He also lives for us within us. Who can make us live like Christ? None except the One who gives the life of Christ to us. As we have the life of Christ, we may bear fruit to the glory of God.

Today, lay these things before God and hope that you may see how God looks upon you and me as being hopeless and helpless. Although you may still hope in yourself as though you are able, God entertains no such expectation since He has already crucified you in Christ. Whenever you take your existence outside of Christ you immediately fall. You should only see yourself in Christ. In Him you are in possession of two facts: namely, having died and been resurrected. The one who lives is he who is in Christ. God wants you to live by the life of Christ. On the other hand, all who are in Adam have died. Lay hold of this fact and you are delivered from the law. Keep in mind that you have not only died to the world, to self and to sin, you have also died to the law so that you will hope no more in yourself but stand firm on the ground which God has given you.

2 The Power of Resurrection

That God hath fulfilled the same unto our children, in that he raised up Jesus; as also it is written in the second psalm, Thou art my Son, this day have I begotten thee. (Acts 13.33)

Cease not to give thanks for you, making mention of you in my prayers; that the God of our Lord Jesus Christ, the Father of glory, may give unto you a spirit of wisdom and revelation in the knowledge of him; . . . that ye may know what is . . . the exceeding greatness of his power to us-ward who believe, according to that working of the strength of his might which he wrought in Christ, when he raised him from the dead, and made him to sit at his right hand in the heavenly places . . .: and he put all things in subjection under his feet, and gave him to be head over all things to the church, which is his body, the fulness of him that filleth all in all. (Eph. 1.16–23)

For in one Spirit were we all baptized into one body . . .; and were all made to drink of one Spirit. (1 Cor.12.13)

Our intention today is to see and understand this matter of the power of resurrection. It is too big a subject to be fully covered in such a short treatment. We only desire to touch upon the central point concerning resurrection. And even in this respect we must hasten to make clear that it is something which no human speech can fully expound upon nor any man's thought can thoroughly grasp. Words and thoughts are totally inadequate in the understanding of resurrection, for it is beyond the comprehension of human thoughts and words. We can only look to the Spirit of the Lord that He may grant us revelation and insight.

We must understand one thing before God, which is, that however perfect and good the creation of man is, he has yet to arrive at God's purpose since he does not have God's life. We may say that man's creation is perfect and yet it is not completed. When God created all other things, He created them completed. Only in the creation of man has He not created to completion. True, from one viewpoint, man *is* perfectly created. Even so, the fact of his having had placed before him the tree of the knowledge of good and evil and the tree of life suggests that man is not yet completed in his creation. Man as created is truly a living soul, but he still does not have in him the life that is represented by the tree of life. Let us see that the difference between man and the rest of creation is just here: that all other things, after their being created, had no need of anything having to be added on, since God had required no further demand of them; man, on the other hand, *did* require a further touch after creation—because

God had, and still has, a special purpose for man. And this last touch of which we speak must be actively added on by man himself—which is to say that there needs to be added to him the fruit of the tree of life.

Unfortunately man adds to himself the fruit of the tree of the knowledge of good and evil instead of the fruit of the tree of life. Let us underscore the fact that man as created is not complete since God has yet to obtain the man that is after His eternal plan. Even if he does *not* eat the fruit of the tree of the knowledge of good and evil, man still cannot satisfy God's heart. In other words, whether the fact of his not eating of the tree of life is true of man before or after he eats the fruit of the tree of the knowledge of good and evil, he is nonetheless limited and incomplete. He may attain to the peak of humanity and still be unfinished so far as God's eternal plan concerning him is concerned, for he does not possess the life of God.

Let us recognize that the purpose of God in creating Adam is not simply in His having made him a living soul by having breathed into a piece of fashioned clay. No, this is very inadequate. Man does not yet have the life of God. He has the *created* life all right, but he does not possess the *uncreated* life. He is bound by time and space. He is created to a certain point, but falls short of arriving at God's full design. For this reason, since the time of Adam, God has been working towards obtaining a man in full accordance with His plan. We notice that throughout the entire Old Testament period—ever since the time of Genesis 3 in fact—God had worked incessantly in the lives of Noah,

Abraham, Isaac, Jacob, Joshua, Samuel, David, and others for the sake of accomplishing what He had originally designed. We also perceive how God had actually apprehended those men and was able to finish His work in them. So far as God's purpose in these men is concerned, we may say that they were apprehended by God. But so far as the man whom God designed to obtain in His eternal plan, none of them was sufficient. All these men reached a certain point but then stopped short of the goal.

But then came the New Testament era. The Son of God came to be a man: the Word became flesh. And this is the man whom God had always longed to have. The man whom He had planned to complete is now found. This man is none other than Christ Jesus. Let us always remember that Christ is the man whom God had continually expected through those many years. Christ is the complete man—God's representative man and the typical man.

Nevertheless, while the Lord Jesus Christ was on earth there was restriction to His manhood. Though He was very different from the rest of the people on earth in that He had the divine nature and was a complete man, yet so far as the matter of power was concerned Christ suffered the limitation of a man in that He was restricted by time and space. When the four men brought a man sick of the palsy to see the Lord Jesus, they had to uncover the roof where He was in order to reach His presence (Mark 2.3,4). When the woman who had an issue of blood wished to touch Him, she had to press through the throng before she could do so (Mark 5.25-31). On the other hand, our Lord commended a Roman centurion on his great faith because he answered, "I am not worthy that thou shouldest come under my roof; but only say the word, and my servant shall be healed" (Matt. 8.8). This man knew that he did not need to press through to the Lord's side in order to touch Him, because he recognized the unlimited side of the Lord. Yet so far as the human side of the Lord Jesus went, what He manifested while on earth was rather straitened in character. This does not imply that there was any imperfection in His personality; it only refers to the fact of a restriction in the release of power. He could not have been more perfect in personality, nonetheless, the manifestation of His power does seem to have been somewhat restricted. But after He died and was resurrected the Lord Jesus did arrive at the peak of completeness.

Two

What is resurrection? Resurrection is the fact that God has gotten a man—the kind of man which He had long expected. While our Lord Jesus Christ was on earth He was a perfect man, nevertheless this perfect man was somewhat circumscribed. The man whom God had desired from the foundation of the world is not to be so confined. What God looked for was resurrection. In the resurrection of the Lord Jesus, Christ transcends all limitations. Thereafter nothing can restrict Him anymore. While He lived on earth Christ had the possibility of death. But after His resurrection death could no longer touch Him. Death and the possibility of death are both destroyed by Him. His word to the apostle John long after His resurrection is: "I was dead, and behold, I am alive for evermore" (Rev. 1.18). He will never die again since the possibility of death is destroyed by Him. Men can no more crucify Him; this possibility of death no longer exists. Now this is called resurrection.

Resurrection means that the man whom God in eternity sought to obtain is now found in our Lord! "Thou art my beloved Son, *this day have I begotten thee,*" says God. *This announcement does not refer to Bethlehem; rather, it points to resurrection.* When Christ was born in Bethlehem God was not able to make this announcement; after Christ is resurrected, however, God can publicly say so (see Acts 13.33). Let us therefore remember that even though the Lord Jesus was perfect in nature, character, and conduct while living on earth, He was nonetheless restricted until resurrected. Afterwards, however, all limitations were gone. And thus resurrection signifies that here is a man who has broken through all the limitations of man. The man whom God was always seeking to find is at last found on the day Christ was raised from the dead.

The resurrection of the Lord Jesus is different from the resurrection of other people mentioned in the Bible. For example, in calling Lazarus out of the grave the Lord Jesus recalled Lazarus to his former living situation in the world. Colloquially speaking, Lazarus' soul returned to his body. He was still bound with grave clothes, and unless he were loosened from them he could not walk properly (John 11.44). He was therefore merely restored to his fleshly life. It was a resuscitation—something quite unlike the resurrection of the Lord Jesus. What made Peter and John believe in the resurrection of the Lord? Note that on the first day of the week, after having heard the report of Mary Magdalene, they ran to the tomb, entered in, and saw "the linen cloths lying, and the napkin, that was upon his head, not lying with the linen cloths, but rolled up in a place by itself" (John 20.6–8), and nobody was inside. And hence they believed. Lazarus, on the other hand, was still wrapped in grave clothes; his body was yet bound by cloths. But the Lord was not bound by them; nothing—absolutely nothing—can restrict Him anymore. Before His resurrection, He too was subject to restrictions of the flesh and matter. But after His resurrection, He is no longer under restriction; He has broken through the grip of death. No limitation of any kind can hold him back.

One brother has spoken well when he once said this: "To the risen Lord, it is not a matter of His coming or going but a matter of His being seen or not seen." Formerly, He came and He went. Now, He neither comes nor goes. Today it is a case of whether or not we see the Lord, whether or not we have revelation. When people receive revelation, they will see; but when they do not have revelation, they will not see. *With* revelation they will touch the Lord; *without* revelation they will not be able to touch Him. Hence the question is not in the Lord's coming or going, but is in our seeing or not seeing. The problem of coming and going no longer exists since such restrictions are gone, because our Lord has been raised from the dead.

After the resurrection of the Lord Jesus, Thomas had doubt in his heart. He expressed it this way: "Except I shall see in his hands the print of the nails, and put my finger into the print of the nails, and put my hand into his side, I will not believe"; but the Lord said, "Be not faithless, but believing"; and after Thomas answered with "My Lord and my God", the Lord said to him: "Because thou hast seen me, thou hast believed: blessed are they that have not seen, and yet have believed" (John 20.24–29). Today it is no longer a matter of our touching Him with the hand, it is a touching Him with faith. And whoever has faith shall touch Him. Christ is today the Lord of resurrection; therefore His former straitened situation is past. We must use faith to touch this risen Lord. If we believe, we shall see Him. It is not because He is not present; rather, our naked eyes are unable to see Him. Today neither time nor space is any longer a problem. Although the greatest limitation with human beings is time and space, in our day these things cannot stand in the way of our Lord. Consequently, the current question is whether we believe. Whenever we look at the Lord with the eye of faith we shall see Him.

The story in John 11 of the raising of Lazarus from the dead gives us much helpful understanding. We may recall the moment Martha saw the Lord. She declared to Him: "Lord, if thou hadst been here, my brother had not died" (v.21). The Lord said to her,

"Thy brother shall rise again" (v.23). How did Martha respond? "I know this will happen at the last day," she said. Being a Jewess, she believed what the Jews held concerning the resurrection at the last day. The Lord therefore declared to her: "I am the resurrection, and the life" (v.25). In the mind of Martha, resurrection and the last day are joined in one; but the Lord shows us that with His being here, the problem of the last day no longer exists. Since He is the resurrection and He is here, the matter of time is past. In resurrection neither time nor space nor any other limitation constitutes a problem.

Our Lord is risen. When the disciples met behind closed doors Jesus came into their midst and manifested himself to them. He could enter without opening the door (see John 20.19, 26). He also appeared to the two disciples on their way to Emmaus. And just as they began to recognize Him, He vanished from their sight (Luke 24.31). This is the marvel of resurrection. He has transcended time, He has transcended space. In just one second He can touch the ends of the earth from here or wherever. No longer can it be said that it will take three to five years to do a certain work or eight to ten years of prayer for a certain thing to happen. What can be said instead is that here is One who transcends time and space. He is the risen Lord.

Christ lived on earth for thirty-odd years. Humanly speaking, he advanced in wisdom and stature (Luke 2.52). But, after He is resurrected He demonstrates the perfect power of God. This power has already broken through the greatest limitation of all—which is death. His life transcends time and space. His life breaks through death. Hence, He is the Living One. Human beings are limited by death, but our Lord is not subject to such limitation. This is the resurrection of our Lord.

We all realize that death is a great limitation. All living things come to an end at death. Be it a blade of grass or a tree, its greatest limitation is death. A dog or a cat may be our pet for three, five, or a few more years. It is very clever and quite useful. But it cannot live on forever. Its life is limited. It is finished at death. And the same is true with human beings. No matter how capable the foolish rich man planned ahead, we read how "God said unto him, Thou foolish one, this night is thy soul required of thee; and the things which thou hast prepared, whose shall they be?" (Luke 12.16–20) When death comes, one loses all. When one is living he may do many things and make himself very useful, but his usefulness ceases with death. As regards the Lord, however, death no longer exists. It is broken through by the Lord. Death cannot hold Him in—for this holding is limitation; and resurrection has thrust aside this greatest of all limitations. Neither gate nor city nor mountain can block resurrection. Neither yesterday, nor today, nor tomorrow can arrest resurrection. Our Lord is not just living, he in fact dies no more. He not only will not die, He also has no possibility of dying. He is the Living one; and He was dead, but He is now alive forevermore (Rev. 1.18). For Him, all limitations have truly passed away.

Resurrection is the power of God: "According to that working of the strength of his might which he wrought in Christ, when he raised him from the dead, and made him to sit at his right hand in the heavenly places, far above all . . . not only in this world, but also in that which is to come" (Eph. 1.19–21). After His resurrection the Lord sits at the right hand of the Father, far above all. He is far above every name that is named. He is far above all in this world as well as in the world to come. The man whom God had planned to have but had failed to apprehend since the foundation of the world is now found in the Lord Jesus after His resurrection. What God looked forward to possess was a man who would be like Him. Before this became factual, He had not gotten whom He had planned for. The God who is is indeed far above all, but He also wants a man to be far above all. Until there is a man who is far above all, God's purpose is not fulfilled. After our Lord was raised from the dead He was received to the Father's right side. Not only the restriction of death is abolished, but all other limitations are overcome. And God has now obtained the man of His plan.

We need to see that the Lord Jesus came to be a representative man. His life on earth for thirty-odd years is representative, and so is His life after resurrection representative in nature. What He represents on earth during those thirty and more years is the moral standard of man—or more accurately, God's moral demand on man. What He expresses to His disciples in the forty days after His resurrection is the power God will give us. So that on the one hand the Lord Jesus represents God's ideal man who reflects the proper moral and spiritual conditions which God requires of man. Should He have come to this world and not died for us nor atoned for our sins, the Lord by so coming would have condemned us because we have all come short of the glory of God. He alone is a man who has the glory of God and who has satisfied God's glory. He is the ideal person. By comparison, we are all sinners and are all unqualified, because He is the moral standard for every one of us. On the other hand, after His resurrection the Lord Jesus represents even more the ideal man of God. We have already commented that when God said "Thou art my Son, this day have I begotten thee" it did not refer to the birth at Bethlehem but to resurrection. On that very same day the Lord Jesus said to Mary Magdalene, "Go unto my brethren, and say to them, I ascend unto my Father and your Father, and my God and your God" (John 20.17). This indicates to us that our becoming sons of God also commences at resurrection.

God needs not only moral people but also powerful people. People having a proper standard of morality cannot alone satisfy God's heart; they also need to possess tremendous power in order to satisfy Him. Since the day He was born in Bethlehem, the Lord Jesus never once came short of the glory of God. This shows that He is a moral person of the highest standard. But after His resurrection—that is, from the time God said "Thou art my Son, this day have I begotten thee"—He manifests also the other side of His personality, He is a man of power. Hereafter there is no question of time and space, nor a question of any kind. The entire problem lies in whether or not people can see.

Oh! Resurrection is such a profound thing that what we are saying here is merely touching its surface!

Three

Acts 2 shows us clearly what resurrection is. It also reveals to us what is the Holy Spirit. Resurrection rids us of the imprisonment of death. The Lord of resurrection transcends all things. What, then, is the Holy Spirit? As the Lord Jesus was raised from the dead, He was exalted by the right hand of God to be seated at God's right hand. As he arrived at the right hand of the Father, He poured forth the Holy Spirit. And hence we can rightly say that the power of the Holy Spirit is the power of resurrection. The Lord locates resurrection and its power in the Holy Spirit who in turn brings it down to earth. Today we have no way to separate resurrection from the Holy Spirit. Whoever encounters the Holy Spirit encounters resurrection. That which was poured forth from heaven on the day of Pentecost and which the disciples saw and heard is the Holy Spirit. Why was the Holy Spirit given? To testify that the Lord has been resurrected. Does the Holy Spirit testify only in words. No, everyone who has met the Holy Spirit knows that the Lord Jesus has risen.

When the Lord was on earth some had leaned on His bosom, some had received things from His hand, some had touched the border of His garment, some had had their feet washed by Him, some had had their bodies raised by Him, and had had their eyes anointed by Him with spittle and clay. Today, though, he is risen—He is in the Spirit. The Lord whom we now may see is what those who had touched Him or were touched by Him on earth could not see. He whom we see today surpasses the One whom they saw on earth. For today we have met the Lord of resurrection. Those who knew the Lord Jesus on earth might say He advanced in wisdom and stature. They might recall how they met Him when he was only 12 years of age or when He was 30 years old. They might relate His history, who his brothers were, and who were His parents. But the Lord we now meet transcends this being "advanced in wisdom and stature": He transcends all boundaries; even the last boundary—death—has He also transcended.

How can the church continue on for nearly two thousand years? Because there are always people who see the Lord of resurrection. For almost 20 centuries, here and there are many saints whose inner state is bright because they have seen the Lord inwardly. We acknowledge that we are not as clear towards the outward Christ as were those people who lived in the age of the Four Gospels. We do not see what they saw. We do not know, as they did, the exact appearance of the Lord in the flesh. Nevertheless, our knowledge of Him today is clearer than those people in the time of the Four Gospels. Our inner state is much brighter than theirs. We have touched the Lord inwardly.

What does the Holy Spirit do on earth today? He communicates the risen Christ to men. If anyone should say he knows the Holy Spirit but not resurrection we will answer that this is impossible. For today this Christ transcends all space, time, death, and every limitation. The Holy Spirit is that Spirit who has raised the Lord Jesus from the dead. The power of the Holy Spirit is therefore the power of resurrection. Wherever the work of the Holy Spirit is, there is the manifestation of the power of resurrection. Where the Holy Spirit is, there is resurrection.

Four

"And he put all things in subjection under his feet, and gave him to be head over all things to the church, which is His body, the fulness of him that filleth all in all" (Eph. 1.22,23). Do we see what the church is? While the Lord Jesus was still living on earth He was the perfect man, but He was yet to be the Head of the church. For at that time He himself was still under restriction, and the possibility of death continued to be on Him because He had not as yet broken the power of death. Had the church become His body at that time, the church would have likewise come under such restriction. Not until the Lord Jesus is risen from the dead does he become the Head of the church and the church become His body. But now, just as He has transcended all things, so too does the church transcend all things. It is true that while the Lord was on earth He was full of power. If we possessed only the power which He possessed while on earth we might perhaps feel sufficient, but God considers it inadequate. Having broken the greatest limitation of all which is death, the Lord Jesus is resurrected. And God puts all things in subjection under His feet and makes Him Head over all things to the church. Thus the church becomes His body. Only after the Lord is resurrected does the church become His body. And thus the Head and the body share the same nature; they are completely one. As the Head is far above all, so the church is far above all. As Christ is beyond any limitation, so the church is beyond any limitation.

With respect to ourselves individually, we of course are still in the flesh; we are therefore subject to the restrictions of space and time. But so far as the nature of the church is concerned, she is the body of Christ—the fullness of Him who fills all in all. She is the vessel for the resurrection life of Christ; hence she may experience the power of Christ's resurrection. May we continually remember this, that "we have this treasure in earthen vessels, that the exceeding greatness of the power may be of God, and not from ourselves" (2 Cor. 4.7). On the one hand we cannot deny we are only useless earthen vessels; but on the other hand we must also see that since God has given us the resurrection life of Christ, faith calls us to experience this power of resurrection. Church history tells us how the church has experienced this resurrection power—here a little and there a little. It may further be said that the church is being built up on the foundation of resurrection. So that one day the saints shall be raptured, their bodies shall be redeemed, and then shall they fully and perfectly manifest this power of resurrection.

A brief survey of church history during the first century might be helpful in this matter. In that first century the gospel was spread by a few Galilean fishermen. According to their personal conditions they were unlearned common people with little courage. Consider Peter, for example. Though he was the strongest among the twelve disciples, yet on the night of the betrayal of the Lord he dared to follow only at a distance. After his arrival at the courtyard of the high priest he could not stand the inquisition of a slave girl and so denied the Lord three times. This amply proves that he was as weak and cowardly as the other disciples. Nevertheless, when Pentecost came and the Holy Spirit descended, Peter and the eleven apostles stood up to speak. He no longer acted like a timid and unlearned fisherman.

Furthermore, the apostles performed many wonders and signs (Acts 2.43). When they were persecuted by the priests, the captain of the temple, and the Sadducees—the twelve having been seized, threatened and forbidden to proclaim the resurrection of the Lord Jesus—their response was: "We cannot but speak the things which we saw and heard"; and they were so bold for the word of the Lord that when the people who judged them "had perceived that they were unlearned and ignorant men, they marvelled" (Acts 4.1–21). They had been transformed from weakness to strength. The reason is none other than that they had known the power of the resurrection of Christ. They no longer lived by their natural life. They lived by the power of that resurrection.

Again, when Stephen was stoned by the people for the sake of the word of the Lord, he had no animosity against them and instead cried out with a loud voice: "Lord, lay not this sin to their charge" (Acts 7.60). Such power comes from resurrection life.

When Paul and Silas were cast into the inner prison they neither despaired nor fainted in heart. Instead of moaning and weeping they "were praying and singing hymns unto God" (Acts 16.25). As a result, the entire household of the jailor believed in God. Such power is truly the manifestation of the power of the resurrection of Christ in their lives.

Even so, to know the power of resurrection requires revelation. How we need the prayer of Ephesians 1: "That the God of our Lord Jesus Christ, the Father of glory, may give unto you a spirit of wisdom and revelation in the knowledge of him; . . . that ye may know what is . . . the exceeding greatness of his power to us-ward who believe, according to that working of the strength of his might which he wrought in Christ, when he raised him from the dead . . ." Here we are told what kind of power it is that God works in those who believe. It is the power which God wrought in Christ when He raised Him from the dead. In other words, just as God raised Christ from the dead in order that he would not be held by death but instead break through all limitations, so God will manifest the same power to us who believe.

We thank God that the church has actually experienced this resurrection power. Our regeneration is by the resurrection of Jesus Christ from the dead (1 Peter 1.3). When we preach and people accept the gospel, this is the fruit of resurrection. The Lord has declared: "All authority hath been given unto me in heaven and on earth" (Matt. 28.18). He has also stated that "where two or three are gathered together in my name, there am I in the midst of them" (Matt. 18.20). If two or three shall agree on earth as touching anything, they may also manifest this power of resurrection. Whether it is regeneration or spiritual growth or godly exercise, it is all a demonstration of resurrection power (see Rom. 8). We know from 1 Corinthians 15 that the secret of Paul's having "labored more abundantly" (v.10) and having been able to "die daily" (v.31) is in resurrection (the theme of the entire chapter). Does not Paul reiterate the same idea in 2 Corinthians 11 by saying: "In labors more abundantly, in prisons more abundantly, in stripes above measure, in deaths oft. Of the Jews five times received I forty stripes save one. Thrice was I beaten with rods, once was I stoned, thrice I suffered shipwreck, a night and a day have I been in the deep; in journeyings often, in perils of rivers . . .; in labor and travail, in watchings often, in hunger and thirst, in fastings often, in cold and nakedness. Besides those things that are without, there is that which presseth upon me daily, anxiety for all the churches" (v.23–28). What power sustains him in willingly enduring these things? It is the power of resurrection.

We are further shown in Philippians 3 that the reason why Paul is able to know "the fellowship of his [Christ's] sufferings, becoming conformed unto his death" is in his being able to "know him, and the power of his resurrection" (v.10).

Among God's children we can discern a great many similar experiences. Some may be in sickness, but they are able to lift up their heads and praise the Lord when they know this power of resurrection. Some may—at the moment of intense pain, tribulation and humiliation which naturally speaking is "beyond their power"—find strength to endure because of the power of resurrection. Just as the Scripture says, "We are pressed on every side, yet not straitened; perplexed, yet not unto despair" (2 Cor. 4.8). All these experiences prove one fact, which is that "the exceeding greatness of the power may be of God, and not from ourselves" (2 Cor. 4.7).

May we continually keep in mind that whatever is the nature of the Head will be the nature of the body. We must ask God to give us a spirit of wisdom and revelation so that we may experience the power of resurrection, for the church ought to enjoy the resurrection power of God on earth. The resurrection life of Christ is already in us. We should ask the Lord to open our eyes that we may know the strength of His might in us. We should be strong in the power of this resurrection. Then shall we be delivered from today's feebleness, inability, self-love, self-pity, and the flesh. We may transcend all these things without being entangled, influenced, and limited.

How immense is resurrection. We can neither express it fully in words nor understand it completely in thoughts. Nevertheless, may the God of peace, who brought again from the dead the Great Shepherd of the sheep through the blood of an eternal covenant—even our Lord Jesus—grant to His church the spirit of wisdom and revelation abundantly, so that the church may know Christ and the power of His resurrection. Amen.